Dr. Memon Salim Karim

DEGREE IN HAND VISION ON HOLD

REDEFINING COMMERCE EDUCATION

Dr. Salim Karim Memon is an educator with over 25 years of experience at the University of Mumbai. Known as "Accounts Baba" for his ability to simplify Accountancy, he has profoundly impacted thousands of students by fostering trust and connection. His work extends beyond teaching; he focuses on understanding student mindsets and the education system's influence on their paths. Through his initiative "Degree In Hand, Vision On Hold: Redefining Commerce Education," he aims to inspire change and promote learning as a journey of clarity and purpose, advocating for an education system that nurtures both knowledge and vision.

First Edition: January 2026
Printed in India

Typeset in Garamond
ISBN: 978-93-6070-663-0

Cover Design: Dr. Memon Salim Karim

STORYMIRROR
Stories that reflect you

Publisher:	StoryMirror Infotech Pvt. Ltd. Unit No-F/705, 7th Floor Kailas Corporate Lounge, Veer Savarkar Road, Vikhroli Park Site, Vikhroli West, Mumbai-400079, Maharashtra, India.
Web:	storymirror.com
Facebook:	@storymirror
Instagram:	@storymirror
Twitter:	@story_mirror
Contact Us:	marketing@storymirror.com

PREFACE

I have spent more than two decades teaching commerce students and working closely with parents, teachers and the education system. During this journey, I have seen dreams take shape and I have also seen dreams quietly fade away. I have seen students who entered the commerce stream with big hopes, but somewhere along the way, their vision went missing. This book was born from those moments.

Every year, I meet hundreds of students. I see the bright eyes of beginners, full of energy and expectation, and I see the tired eyes of final-year students, unsure of where they are headed. I also meet parents who want the best for their children but often do not know what the "BEST" really means. After all these years, one truth has become very clear to me. The way we teach and prepare our students is not enough. It needs to change.

With the introduction of the National Education Policy 2020, many believe that transformation is already happening. But the real question is, are we moving in the right direction or are we simply repainting an old wall and calling it new? This book is my honest attempt to explore that question.

It is not filled with academic theories or long policy discussions. It is filled with real experiences. The stories you will read are about students I have taught, teachers I have worked with and the challenges I have personally faced in a system that often resists change. Every teacher will recognise these stories, and every student will see a part of themselves in them.

In these pages, you will discover:

Why many students choose commerce, and why some never really choose it at all.

What parents think about commerce, and what they should be thinking.

The kind of teachers our system produces, and the kind we truly need.

How the education system runs today, and how it should run tomorrow.

I am not here to blame anyone. I am a part of this system too. I am simply putting my thoughts, experiences and questions on the table for readers to reflect upon, discuss and maybe act upon. I promise that this is not a boring lecture in the form of a book. It is a journey filled with moments that will make you smile, nod in agreement and sometimes shake your head in disbelief.

By the time you finish reading, I hope you will not only understand commerce education better but also begin to see the entire system in a new light. And perhaps, when education truly begins to transform, I will return with another book, not about what went wrong but about what finally went right.

Dr. Salim Karim Memon

Educationist, Researcher and Guide

ACKNOWLEDGMENT

"*Some journeys are not written with ink, but with gratitude.*"

Every book has a beginning. Some begin with a moment of inspiration, others with a quiet thought. This one began with a single question that refused to stay silent. *Can one voice really make a difference in an entire system?* I did not have the answer then. But what I did have were people who walked beside me, who believed in me even when I questioned myself.

My first and deepest thanks go to **Dr. Dinesh Sanadhi.** He did not just encourage me to write this book; he planted the first seed of confidence in my mind. Every idea needs someone who believes in it before the world does. For me, that someone was him.

To my parents, **Abdul Karim Memon** and **Raziya Karim Memon,** your love is the soil from which every part of my journey has grown. You gave me strength when I was weak, faith when I doubted myself, and courage when I stood alone. Everything I am began with both of you.

To Javed Karim Memon and Shahid Karim Memon, and their families, thank you for standing behind me with quiet strength. Every dream looks bigger and brighter when your people believe in you, even when you are still learning to believe in yourself.

To my wife, Farhana Memon, and my children, Nawaz Memon and Safa Memon, your patience, love, and quiet sacrifices gave me the peace and purpose to stay the course. You are my constant source of strength. As a proud student of University of Mumbai, I learned early that real strength often begins quietly — in classrooms that shape more than just minds.

To my friends, thank you for being the quiet walls that never let me fall. You brought laughter when things were heavy and strength when words were few.

A very special thanks to my partner in crime, **Shahbaz Sastikar**. A friend, a brother, and my loudest cheerleader in silence. Some people do not just support you, they become your story. He is one of them.

To my colleagues and the team at St. Joseph College of Arts & Commerce and Shah K.M. College, thank you for sharpening my thoughts through your conversations, ideas, and belief in my work. Every push, even the quiet ones, left a lasting mark.

To my teachers, thank you for lessons that no textbook ever carried. Your influence continues to shape me every single day I step into a classroom.

And to everyone who has stood by me, often without being seen, thank you. Some hands guide you quietly, some voices push you forward softly, and some hearts simply stay with you. This book belongs to all of you.

My team at Zean Coaching Classes will always be a part of who I am. They are not just a part of this journey; they are the roots that keep it grounded and strong.

If gratitude were a story, then every chapter would carry the voice of someone who stood with me. This acknowledgment is not a list of thanks. It is a map of hearts that carried me when my steps were small.

With love, respect, and a quiet smile,

Dr. Salim Karim Memon

TABLE OF CONTENTS

CHAPTER 1

THE FIRST STEP INTO CONFUSION

"Congratulations, beta! You're now a COMMERCE GRADUATE."

Let's get one thing clear from the start:

This book is not about the rare few who chose commerce out of deep passion or purpose. This is not for the ones who dreamt of becoming investment bankers at 13 or were solving GST problems while the rest of us were struggling with fractions. **No.**

This is for the masses, not the classes. For the students who took commerce not because they were clear but because it was convenient.

Let's be honest:

Most commerce students didn't enter this stream with stars in their eyes.

They entered with lines like:

"Science is too risky."

"Arts are for creative people. Are you creative? No. So take commerce."

"Your percentage fits only in commerce. Be realistic."

"The college is nearby. Take commerce. No travelling."

"You'll be a graduate. That's enough for a good marriage."

"Take commerce now. We'll see about CA later." (Spoiler: they never see CA later.)

And my personal favorite is:

"Don't think too much. Everyone is taking commerce."

In India, career choices are often made like wedding buffet items—not what you love, but what's available, affordable, and commonly served. And so, students land in commerce without a clue, and three years later, graduate with a degree in one hand… and a big question mark in the other.

This book is for them.

For the students who spent more time searching for project topics than understanding what commerce really is. For the ones who memorized business definitions, but never understood how to start one. For the teachers, parents, and policymakers who think commerce is "SIMPLE."

(Yes, simple enough to confuse lakhs of students every year.)

We're not here to glorify success stories.

We're here to unpack the confusion.

Because somewhere between "TAKE COMMERCE" and *"Now what?"* lies a whole generation stuck in a system that forgot to give it vision.

So if you've ever wondered:

"Why am I studying this?"

"Will this get me a job?"

"Is everyone else as lost as I am?"

The answer is in these pages.

This is your story.

Let's begin.

The Story That Opened My Eyes

The story I am about to share is not just an incident; it is a mirror that reflects the true condition of our commerce education. It happened not too long ago in my own office. I had hired a young commerce graduate, full of hope, carrying a degree that declared him 'qualified' in commerce. Three years of college education were behind him. Lectures attended. Exams passed. Certificates earned. One morning, I called him to my desk. I handed him a simple task, something that every commerce student should easily handle.

***"Can you please fill out this bank cheque?"* I asked.**

He took the cheque in his hands. For a few moments, he stared at it. His eyes moved across the blank spaces where the date, amount, and signature needed to be filled. Slowly, his head lifted, and he looked at me—uncertain, nervous, almost frozen. His hands were slightly shaking. I smiled, thinking perhaps it was his first time. To help him gain some confidence, I decided to give him a few more simple banking tasks—deposit a cheque, withdraw some cash, update the passbook, and collect a demand draft. But each time, he returned with confusion written all over his face. He did not know how to fill out simple forms. He was unsure where to go in the bank or whom to talk to. Even the basic steps of banking seemed like a complicated puzzle to him. As I watched him struggle with these everyday tasks, a serious question arose in my mind:

What exactly have we taught him in the name of commerce?

Isn't commerce supposed to prepare students for the world of trade, industry, and finance? If a student feels lost even while performing a simple bank transaction, how can we expect him to understand bigger business concepts? How can we believe that he will be able to handle investments, mutual funds, stock markets, or manage trade and industry? I stood there silently and thought more deeply. Some exceptional students, , no doubt,, manage to learn things on their own. They find ways to fill the gaps left by the system. But my book is not about those few exceptions. I am writing this for the majority—for the common students who form the backbone of our commerce education system.

These are the students who spend years in classrooms, memorize definitions, write exams, and collect degrees. Yet when real-life situations knock on their door, they find themselves helpless, confused, and lost. At that moment, I felt the true pain of our broken system. Commerce education, whose first and basic purpose is to help students understand trade, industry, and commerce, has lost its soul somewhere. If they can't handle a simple bank transaction, how can they ever handle the world of business? This one simple incident made me realize why I must write this book.

Commerce as a stream of education is fundamentally designed to develop a deep understanding of trade, industry, and commerce. According to Chaturvedi (2005), the core objective of commerce education is to equip students with comprehensive knowledge of business operations, economic systems, and the structure of commercial activities. However, despite these well-defined academic goals, commerce education in practice often fails to achieve its intended purpose. The curriculum remains largely theoretical, with minimal emphasis on practical exposure and real-world applications. As a result, a significant number of commerce graduates leave college without gaining even the most basic understanding of how businesses function in reality.

There are alarming examples that illustrate this disconnect. Many commerce graduates, despite spending three years studying business-related subjects, have never opened a bank account by the time they complete their degree. Others are unaware of how to file income tax returns or the significance of financial documents such as PAN cards, GST registrations, and trade licenses. Additionally, most students lack hands-on understanding of trade flows, supply chains, industrial structures, or entrepreneurship in a competitive economy. They may have memorized textbook definitions and theories but remain unequipped to apply this knowledge practically.

This failure of commerce education raises serious concerns. When a graduate cannot perform basic business tasks or navigate financial systems, it questions the effectiveness of the degree. Commerce, as a discipline, promises to prepare students for the dynamic world of trade and business. Yet, without practical implementation, internships, or exposure to real-time industry practices, the education remains hollow. Though the aim of commerce education is noble and ambitious, in its current form, it does not fulfill its promise. It produces degree-holders rather than skilled professionals capable of contributing meaningfully to trade, industry, and commerce.

Commerce education has traditionally been structured to prepare students for employment in business and industry. Shukla (2008) notes that the goal is to build competence for clerical, accounting, managerial, and administrative roles. In this regard, commerce education does fulfill its purpose—many graduates enter these fields and perform the roles they are trained for. However, this raises a critical question:

Is this the only purpose of commerce education?

Should commerce education merely produce job-seekers who fit into existing systems, or should it also aim to create job creators, entrepreneurs, and business leaders? Commerce, by its very nature, involves trade, innovation, and economic development. Yet, the current system falls short in encouraging innovation, risk-taking, and entrepreneurial thinking. If the true potential of commerce is to drive economic progress, then simply preparing students for employment cannot be its ultimate goal. A reimagined approach to commerce education is needed—one that builds leaders for tomorrow's economy.

Commerce education today claims to foster entrepreneurial skills, creativity, and risk-taking abilities. Gupta and Srivastava (2010) argue that commerce education should not only prepare students for employment but also encourage them to develop independent ventures and think innovatively. With the introduction of the National Education Policy (NEP), a new vision was promised—one focused on skill development and entrepreneurship.

Yet, a critical question remains: Has commerce education truly succeeded in instilling an entrepreneurial mindset? The answer appears to be **NO**. Despite policy reforms, the classroom remains rigid, theory-heavy, and exam-oriented. There is little room for business simulations, startup incubation, or creative exploration. As a result, the system continues to produce commerce graduates who seek jobs rather than create them. This shortfall challenges the very promises of the NEP and raises a broader concern: If commerce cannot produce entrepreneurs in today's economy, then what transformation is education truly achieving?

From Classroom to Reality – A Gap Too Wide to Ignore

I have been in this profession for many years, and over time, I have taught thousands of commerce students. But if you ask me, how many of them actually implemented what they were taught in real life? I would say very few. That's the honest truth. Let me give you a simple example. In our commerce curriculum, we teach students how to prepare final accounts in 11th standard, 12th standard, and again at the degree level. We teach formats, adjustments, trading accounts, profit and loss accounts, balance sheets. But here's my serious question: How many ordinary accountants actually prepare final accounts manually today? In the real world, most of them just sit in front of a computer and enter expenses or income into software. The software automatically prepares the statements. So despite teaching final accounts for years, no company is asking fresh graduates to prepare them from scratch. At most, they are asked to enter bills, vouchers, or sales details.

Now think deeper: How many commerce students even enter the accounting field? Many never do. And those who do often find the work is not what they expected. That means what we taught them painstakingly and repeatedly has no real use in their career.

It doesn't stop there. We teach topics like Sole Trading Concern, Partnership Firm, and Joint Stock Company. But how many students ever go on to start a business of their own? How many even consider it? This is where our education system faces a real crisis—a gap between knowing and doing. We teach letter writing, communication skills, and business correspondence. But honestly, all these tasks today can be done using a smartphone and AI-based tools. So what we need to teach students now is how to communicate ideas, how to present with confidence, how to think critically—not just how to draft a letter. Yes, I agree the curriculum has seen some updates in recent years. The New Education Policy (NEP) talks about innovation, creativity, and skill-based learning. It sounds promising. But the real issue is not the content it's the implementation.

Let me talk about Taxation, one of the core subjects. Students are still made to memorize definitions, sections, and legal terms. But even professional Chartered Accountants don't remember all tax laws. They refer to books and digital tools to calculate tax accurately. So why aren't we allowing open-book formats in taxation exams? Wouldn't that bring students closer to real-world practice? We must understand: Times have changed. People don't wait for 5-day Test matches; they prefer fast, action-packed T20 cricket. Similarly, students today need faster, smarter, and more practical ways to learn. They need hands-on experience. They need simulations. They need exposure.

The New Education Policy has taken steps in the right direction. It offers freedom of subject selection across colleges, encourages flexibility, and promotes creativity. But here's the reality: most students don't even understand what NEP offers. They are confused. They're still stuck between outdated patterns and modern promises. Earlier, students had 6 subjects. Now they are offered 10 or 11. They are not at all clear with Minor, Major, etc. But more subjects don't always mean more clarity. They need guidance, not just choices.

In this book, I will explore these real-life issues that I have observed personally as a teacher and mentor. I will talk about:

The broken link between theory and practice

The role of parents and their expectations

The teachers of the system

The policymakers and their blind spots

The student's own confusion and lack of direction and his responsibilities as a student

And how we can bring back meaning into lectures, classrooms, and careers

Let me be clear this book is not to criticize anyone. It is not against the system. It is a wake-up call to change the way we think. It is a voice for the students who sit quietly in classrooms, complete his or her assignments, and walk out with degrees but no direction. My only aim is to change the thinking. If I can make one parent think, one teacher reflect, or one student awaken to their own potential then this book has done its job.

From Thought to Reality – The Stories That Follow

Before we move ahead, I want to make one thing clear—this book is not just about what should be taught. It's about what is actually happening. In the next two chapters, I will share real-life stories—some where education empowered, and others where education disappointed. These are not fictional tales. They are real examples—real students, real parents, real decisions, and real consequences. I have seen these stories unfold in front of my eyes. Some of them made me proud. Some left me deeply disturbed. But all of them carry one common thread: they reflect what our education system is doing to young minds today. These stories are not here to blame. They are here to open a conversation. A conversation about the mindset of parents, the confusion of students, the gaps in teaching, and the emotional journey behind every career decision.

Over the years, I have experienced that in commerce stream. Most of them didn't choose commerce out of passion or interest. They chose it because it felt safe. Because it was convenient. Because everyone else was doing it. Or simply because they didn't know what else to choose. *"We think we are steering the ship, but sometimes, we're just drifting with the tide."* That's the reality I see every day as a commerce teacher. In truth, many students don't actively choose commerce. Commerce happens to them. In the chapters ahead, I will introduce you to students who reflect this truth—some who quietly followed the flow, and others who eventually found the courage to swim against it. Their stories are powerful, sometimes painful, and always real. If you're a parent, you might find your child in these pages. If you're a teacher, you might recognize your classroom. If you are already a graduate, you might question yourself, *"What are you because of commerce?"* And if you're a student, you might just find yourself. Let's move forward. Let's meet the faces behind the degrees. The journeys behind the lectures. And the stories that expose not just what went wrong, but also what can still be made right.

CHAPTER 2

UNPLANNED PATHS, UNFORGETTABLE LESSONS

Commerce Without Clarity

This chapter challenges the conventional path of Commerce education in India, where students often enter the stream by default rather than desire. It highlights the disconnect between academic content and real-world applicability and urges a shift from rote learning to experiential, passion-driven learning. Through real-life student stories from cafés to fitness centers, from abroad jobs to local startups, the chapter emphasizes the power of practical exposure, self-belief, and purposeful education. Ultimately, it proposes a more dynamic, entrepreneurial, and student-centered approach to Commerce education where passion meets practice and purpose becomes the true curriculum.

The Default Choice: When Commerce is Taken Without a Clue

Have you ever asked a student, *"Why did you choose Commerce?"*

The answers I've received over the years could fill a comedy script and a psychology report, because the truth is, most students don't choose Commerce with clarity. They don't dream of becoming entrepreneurs, accountants, or economists. They choose it because… well, it was there. In colleges all over the country, Commerce has quietly become the "DEFAULT OPTION." Not the dream, not the plan—just the leftover seat that still feels respectable. It's not chosen out of passion, but out of convenience. And the reasons? Let's just say, they are as confusing as they are entertaining. One student told me, *"My dad asked me to take Commerce."* That's it. No further explanation. I asked, *"Do you enjoy it?"* He said, *"I think so… I mean, I'm trying."* Another said, *"My older brother told me Commerce is safe. You get jobs easily."* When I asked what kind of job he wanted, he replied, *"Any job is fine, sir."* A future built entirely on vague advice. Then there was the student who said, *"I only wanted admission in this college. Commerce was the only seat available, so I took it."* That's like going to a restaurant for pizza and eating whatever they have left because the table looked nice. A girl once smiled and said, *"All my friends took Commerce. We decided we'll be in the same class."* When I asked if she liked the subjects, she paused and said, *"I haven't really thought about it yet. But at least I'm not alone."* Imagine choosing a career path because your group chat voted for it. Another boy confidently said, *"I heard Commerce has fewer lectures, more holidays, and a lot of college events. It sounded like a good life balance."* He didn't mention anything about learning finance or business—he just wanted a chilled-out routine. And the most unexpected one? A student looked me straight in the eye and said, *"I chose Commerce because I liked the college uniform."* For a moment, I wasn't sure if I should laugh or counsel him. His entire academic future was based on fabric choice. But these aren't just jokes.

These are real answers from real students. They reflect a very real problem. Commerce—a stream that teaches you how the world functions, how businesses operate, how money moves—is being taken up by students who have never asked themselves a single serious question about their own goals. They've never explored what commerce really offers. They haven't thought about what they want to do after graduation. They just show up, take notes, pass exams, and hope life will figure itself out. And that's the biggest danger—not confusion, but blind acceptance. When students step into a stream without purpose, they wander through it without passion. And when that happens, even the best syllabus feels empty.

Commerce deserves better. It deserves students who are curious, creative, and committed. It needs minds that are excited to understand business, economics, and finance, not just looking for the easiest option.

If we want to change the future of commerce education, we must begin at the start—by helping students ask the right questions before they choose. Not *"Where are my friends going?"* Not *"What did my cousin take?"* But *"What do I want to learn? What do I want to build? What excites me?"*

Because a stream chosen with clarity becomes a career built with confidence.

When Budget Chooses the Stream

One day, a father walked into my cabin along with his son. The boy had bright, sharp eyes, a confident posture, and a strong interest in biology. As we started the discussion, I casually asked, *"Have you considered putting him in science? Maybe he could become a doctor?"* The father smiled. Not the kind of smile that says yes, but the kind that hides a thousand calculations. He quietly pulled out a small folder from his bag. Inside it were sheets neatly handwritten and color-coded. He started reading:

"To become a doctor, sir, admission fees: ₹10 lakhs minimum. Coaching and entrance preparation: ₹3 lakhs. Hostel and living costs for 5 years: ₹15 lakhs. Books, practical kits, extra charges: another ₹2 lakhs. That's over ₹30 lakhs, sir, for a medical seat."

He flipped the page.

"Engineering is better, but still not cheap. Good colleges demand ₹2 to ₹3 lakhs per year. Add coaching, transportation, hostel, and daily expenses – another ₹8 to ₹10 lakhs over four years."

He then took out a final paper.

"Now, sir, this is my budget. I run a small business. I can afford ₹30,000 per year. That's it."

He looked at me not with helplessness, but with quiet acceptance. *"That's why he's in Commerce, sir. Not because he doesn't love science. But because I can't afford to let him love it."* That moment stayed with me. We often talk about interest, aptitude, dreams, but sometimes, dreams come with price tags. And for middle-class families, Commerce is not just a stream – it's a lifeline. It's affordable. It fits the budget. It offers flexibility. And it allows families to educate their children without drowning in debt. I've seen so many students in Commerce who actually wanted to become architects, researchers, pilots, doctors. But between talent and tuition, tuition wins. Between passion and pocket, pocket decides. Commerce is not just a subject people walk into – sometimes, it's the only door open. And the irony? Many of these students who never intended to be in Commerce turn out to be some of the most successful business minds later. Because they learn something precious that no course guarantees: how to make the best out of what you have.

The Degrees Without Direction

Two years of junior college; three years plus six semesters; countless lectures, assignments, submissions, events, and exams. That's the typical journey of a Commerce student in college. On paper, it sounds well-structured. Every year has a plan. There are theory subjects, occasional industrial visits, college festivals, academic competitions, and even sports meets. From the outside, the system looks active, functional, and moving.

But here's the uncomfortable truth: the structure may exist, but the direction often doesn't.

Ask any teacher, *"What do students aim for during their Commerce degree?"* and you'll likely hear, *"They just want to pass."* not to learn deeply, not to build anything, just to pass.

Education has quietly become a checklist:

Submit the assignments.

Appear for the exams.

Collect passing marks.

Get certificates for participation.

Repeat until graduation.

I once had a student who proudly brought me a file full of certificates — seminars attended, workshops joined, sports events played. I asked, *"This is great, but what did you learn from them?"* He smiled awkwardly and said, *"Sir, it looks good for placements."* That was the goal — not growth, not clarity — just a resume that looks ready. By the time students reach their final year, the entire conversation shifts. Now it's all about placements. Not purpose. Not passion. Just: *"Where will I get a job?"* and *"How much will they pay?"* Colleges respond by organizing job fairs, soft-skill workshops, and crash courses on cracking interviews. Companies come, interviews happen, and a few students get selected. The rest? They either disappear quietly or get lost in the chaos of uncertainty. And here lies the irony: Placement numbers are treated like trophies, posted proudly on college notice boards and websites. But no one talks about the quality of those jobs. No one asks if the student is actually excited about the job they've accepted, or if they even understand it. One of my ex-students was placed in a sales job at a finance firm. He was happy for two weeks. Then the stress began. The targets were impossible. The job had no connection to what he had studied for three years. Eventually, he left and started freelancing in digital marketing — something he had learned on his own through YouTube, not his curriculum. *"Sir,"* he once told me, *"I wish college had helped me figure out who I am instead of just preparing me for some job I never liked."* Another student had a brilliant startup idea during her third year. She wanted to start a small organic product brand online. She approached a faculty member for guidance. The response? *"Focus on placements. Business can wait."* So she parked her idea and sat for interviews. She got a job. Six months later, she quit. Today, she runs that very brand she once paused, and it's doing better than she imagined. So yes, we are producing job seekers. But are we building job creators? Are we encouraging risk-takers, innovators, entrepreneurs? Or just pushing students toward whatever vacancy happens to be available? But that investment must be meaningful. It must have direction. Otherwise, a degree becomes just a paper, not a purpose. Commerce has the potential to create bold, brilliant thinkers. But when the system focuses only on exams and placements, it forgets its deeper goal: to shape minds that not only find jobs but also create them.

The Forgotten Entrepreneur

Let me tell you a story that repeats itself in quiet corners of every college campus. There was a student I once taught who had fire in his eyes and a notebook full of ideas. He wanted to start his own business—an online marketplace for handmade local products. He had researched suppliers, planned his website, and even thought of a brand name. Every conversation with him was filled with enthusiasm. You could tell—this guy was wired for entrepreneurship. But in his final year, the placement season arrived. And so did a "RESPECTABLE" job offer from a finance firm. Nothing too exciting, but it came with a decent salary, free coffee, and a big brand name. His parents were thrilled. His friends clapped. Everyone said, *"Congratulations! This is success!"*

What happened next?

The business plan was gently folded and tucked into the back of a drawer. He told himself, *"Maybe next year… once I settle down a bit."* Weeks turned into months. The startup became a story he told at parties—*"You know, I once had this idea…"* This is not an isolated case. It happens all the time. It's not because students lack dreams. It's not because they aren't capable. It's because we have created a system that celebrates security over self-belief. A system where job offers are seen as medals, and business ideas are treated like distractions. A system where even the most passionate entrepreneur is gently pushed toward a 9-to-5 routine because "IT'S SAFER." And let's be honest—budget plays a huge role too. Many students have the hunger to build something, but not the financial cushion to take risks. I remember one student who had a brilliant food truck idea. But when I asked him why he didn't pursue it, he replied, *"Sir, I already owe my dad one lakh for last semester's fees. He's not in the mood to fund a truck right now."* Fair enough. Another student joked, *"If I say I'm starting my own business, my family won't take it seriously. They'll just think I'm sitting at home, doing nothing, using the internet all day—basically, jobless."* It may sound funny, but it's painfully real. Budget often becomes the silent killer of bold ideas. Not every student can afford to take a leap. So when a job offer arrives, even if it's not what they truly want, they grab it—not with excitement, but with a sigh of relief. And just like that, another entrepreneur is lost to the comfort zone.

Degrees Alone Don't Serve Success—But a Combo Meal Might

Let me tell you about one of my students. A boy who didn't just attend college — he lived two lives each day. Every morning, he came to college and attended his commerce lectures like any other student. But after the last bell rang, he rushed to a café where he worked part-time. His job wasn't glamorous — he cleaned tables, managed small orders, interacted with customers, and helped with basic stock-keeping. Nothing fancy, but everything real. While commerce textbooks taught him about businesses, that café gave him a chance to see one in action. As months passed, something amazing started happening. His responsibilities grew. He was not just cleaning anymore — he began managing shifts, dealing with vendors, resolving customer complaints, and even learning how inventory is handled in real time. It was like watching a commerce syllabus come alive without exams, without fear of failure, and without waiting for final results.

After graduation, he didn't go job-hunting. He went dream-hunting. With help from a local financier, and armed with both his degree and his practical experience, he opened his own restaurant. And guess what? It worked. Now here's the point we all must think about:

His **DEGREE** gave him **THEORY**.

His **PART-TIME JOB** gave him **PRACTICAL**

EXPERIENCE.

But it was his **PASSION** that gave him **DIRECTION.**

Let's not ignore this powerful formula:

Commerce + Real Experience + Personal Passion = Real Education

Had he only studied commerce, he might still be job-seeking. But because he lived the combination, he became a job-creator. Isn't it strange that our system still expects students to walk only one road at a time? You either study or you work. You either earn or you learn. You either attend classes or you explore your calling. But why not both? Why not a model where education is a combination, not a compromise? Why not let commerce meet creativity, theory meet exposure, and passion meet purpose? The New Education Policy is hinting at this blended future, but we need to accelerate the clarity. We must build a system where students are allowed—even encouraged— to discover themselves outside the classroom while still learning within it.

From Flexing to Flourishing: The Fitness Friends Who Built a Brand

Now let me tell you about another group of students, this time, from a very different world. These were not your regular classroom toppers. In fact, they barely attended lectures. But if you visited the local gym at 6 a.m. or 9 p.m., you'd always find them there lifting, training, sweating, and following a strict diet like professionals. For them, fitness wasn't just a hobby. It was their life.

College? That was just to keep their parents happy.

They came to campus just enough to mark attendance. They sat in a few lectures, gave just enough exams to pass. Their hearts, however, was pounding not for commerce but for curls and cardio. Now, you may wonder: Why are they even in a commerce course? Well, unknowingly, they were doing something brilliant. While college gave them the theory, the gym gave them practical experience, and their heart gave them unshakable passion. I noticed some of them didn't stop at building muscles; they started building skills. They began enrolling in fitness certification programs, learning about anatomy, workout science, personal training, nutrition, and business models around gyms and wellness. By the time they graduated, they weren't looking for jobs. They were ready to open gyms. Some got support from local financiers. Some had parents who saw the spark and invested in their dreams. And soon, these boys who once came to college just for attendance were now running fully operational fitness centers. And here's the best part: They weren't just trainers. They were entrepreneurs. They managed memberships, handled client packages, ran Instagram pages, created diet plans, designed merchandise, and even offered online coaching.

They didn't just flex in front of mirrors. They built a business empire with muscles and marketing.

And once again, the formula was clear:

Commerce gave them a foundation.

Experience gave them expertise.

And passion gave them power

They didn't follow the syllabus; they followed their calling. Now imagine, if our education system had allowed them to combine fitness and commerce officially, and offered a course on fitness entrepreneurship, business planning, or digital wellness branding. They could've been trained earlier, better, and faster. But still, they made it. Not because of what the system gave them, but because of what they built from the gaps. So when people say, *"Only marks matter,"* I say, *"Sometimes, what really matters can't be graded."* This story, like the café student's, proves a simple truth:

Education + Experience + Passion = Real, Working Success

Let's stop choosing just one.

Let's blend them all.

After the café hustlers and fitness freaks, let's now talk about another very special species of students — those who never miss a chance to complain, debate, or file a grievance. You know them.

They're the ones who'll spot a broken fan faster than the teacher spots low attendance. They'll question why the chalk is too small, why the mic isn't working, and even why the peon gave them a weird look. These are the students who were born with a megaphone in their throat and a complaint register in their brain. They don't just talk. They roar. Every timetable change? Protest. Every rule update? Objection. Every missing attendance mark? They will file an RTI! And of course, they never walk alone. One raises a voice and six more follow as if a rally had just broken out in the corridor. You could literally feel as if elections are happening between

Lecture Room No. 2 and the washroom! Even their own friends would sigh and say.

"Yaar, tumhe kya zarurat hai? Apna attendance lagao aur niklo na!"

But guess what? These weren't just drama queens (and kings). They were future politicians in training.

They didn't waste time. They were investing in their real calling: Leadership. Today, many of them are leaders in student councils, youth political wings, NGOs, and even mainstream parties. They knew how to spot problems, rally people, negotiate, debate, and most importantly, stay loud without being thrown out (well, most of the time). And the best part? They also studied commerce!

So now they're not just shouting in rallies; they're reading budgets, analyzing votes like balance sheets, and running campaigns like corporate events. One such example is Aditya Thackeray, a commerce graduate who didn't just go to college to sit in class. He was already leading youth movements, speaking on public platforms, and preparing for real politics. And now? He's a national-level political leader with thousands following his voice.

The lesson?

Commerce gave them the system.

College gave them the stage.

Passion gave them the mic and they never gave it back.

These were not your 90%-attendance students.

They were the 90%-resistance ones.

But today, they've turned their energy into real impact.

So before you roll your eyes at that one guy always arguing with the teacher, just pause and ask:

"Is this our future MLA?"

Because honestly, the ones who once fought for cold water in the canteen…

are now fighting for votes in the Vidhan Sabha.

Once again, the formula stands tall:

Education + Exposure + Passion = Powerful People

Just don't forget it's the combination that wins, not the classroom alone.

Let's not just give degrees.

Let's give them direction.

Let's not just build resumes.

Let's build real stories of growth.

Because in the end, only commerce cannot achieve success.

But when you mix commerce with real exposure and a spark of passion, that's when the real magic happens. The Passion – which is always outside the syllabus.

"The only source of knowledge is experience."

The Abroad Effect: From Jobs to Startups

Many students travel abroad after graduation and take up modest jobs waiting tables, managing inventory, or assisting in stores. But these roles teach more than expected. Students learn professionalism, time management, and how real economies function.

Eventually, some return to India not as job seekers, but as confident entrepreneurs. They invest their savings into startups, cafés, salons, and retail stores armed with both knowledge and belief.

What changed?

They understood customer service.

They saw systems in action.

Most importantly, they discovered their own potential.

Commerce gave them a base. The experience gave them belief. Most importantly, they have the required finance for investment and the courage to dare

Commerce gave them a base.

Experience gave them belief.

Finance gave them courage.

The Curriculum We Truly Need

What if our Commerce classrooms also asked:

What excites you?

What can you create?

How can we support your passion?

Alongside accounting and economics, what if we taught:

- Creative thinking
- Customer-focused design

- Business model development
- Risk-taking and resilience
- Startup finance

Then we would not just produce degree holders. We would cultivate confident creators.

A Wake-Up Call, Not a Criticism

This chapter is not a criticism of Commerce education. It is a call to evolve. India doesn't merely need more graduates. It needs entrepreneurial minds, problem-solvers, and visionaries.

Let's reimagine our goals:

From placement to purpose

From memorization to creation

From passing to practicing

Because the real curriculum is not confined to the syllabus, it is shaped by the passions students pursue, the skills they acquire, and the impact they aim to create.

Commerce education should create thinkers and visionaries — not just followers and job-seekers.

But today, many students are still drifting - guided more by external expectations than their own dreams. And this is why I am writing this book.

It is a wake-up call - for:

Parents

Teachers

Policy-makers

Universities

Colleges

"We are not the masters of our journey,

We simply drift wherever the winds may take us."

Because the real curriculum isn't in our books at all—it's in the choices students make when no teacher is watching. Some chase dreams outside classrooms, some settle for comfort zones, and some carry untold battles behind their quiet smiles. If you really want to know where commerce education stands today, don't just read the syllabus, listen to the students. Their stories will surprise you. Some will make you laugh, some will make you pause, and a few might even make you uncomfortable. But each one holds a mirror to the system and to ourselves as teachers, parents, and policymakers. So let's step away from theory for a while. Let's meet the students—not the perfect poster ones, but the real ones. The ones who drifted in, stumbled around, and still taught us lessons no textbook ever could.

CHAPTER 3

BEYOND BOOKS: LESSONS FROM LIFE

Before we move ahead, I want to pause and share something real. What you're about to read next doesn't come from textbooks, research, or reports. It comes from my day-to-day experience as a teacher, watching students walk into the commerce stream with all kinds of reasons, but very little clarity. Some students join commerce because science looked too hard. Some enter because their friends chose it. A few just follow what their parents tell them. One student even told me, *"Sir, I didn't plan anything. I just took admission and thought I'll see what happens."* That one sentence says so much about the confusion many students carry. Over the years, I've come across many such students. Some are regular in class but don't know what subject they're learning. Some are good at heart but never submit assignments. Some are smart but completely disconnected from the stream. They are not weak students. They are simply unclear, directionless, and unsure why they are here. That's why I decided to share these real-life stories. Some will connect directly to the message of this book. Some are simply here to record what I've observed over the years. They may sound funny or even strange, but they are all true. These stories reflect what happens when students enter a stream without proper guidance or understanding. Commerce is a great field, but if the entry is confused, the journey often remains confused. Through these stories, I hope you will understand what students are really going through—not just what they write in exams. So now, let's meet the students. Not the ones from motivational posters, but the real ones—the ones still figuring things out, just like many of us once did.

The Unexpected Entrepreneur: My Own Story

I wasn't born to be an entrepreneur. In fact, for a long time, I didn't even believe I could be one. I barely scraped through school, scoring just 57.57% in my Class 10 exam under the Maharashtra Board. Back then, that was considered low. Like many middle-class students, my biggest dream wasn't to build a business; it was simply to find a stable job and survive. I remember feeling invisible in the education system, just another face in the crowd, told to study hard and get a good job. Entrepreneurship was never mentioned. It was like a secret path only meant for a lucky few. My father ran a small imitation jewellery business, but even he discouraged me from joining. "AIM HIGHER," he said. *"Don't settle for small-scale trading."* So, I followed the script. I didn't wake up one morning with a dream of becoming an entrepreneur. There was no lightning bolt of inspiration or dramatic moment of awakening. My story began like most middle-class students in India, quietly, with average marks and absolutely no clue what I wanted to do in life. In school, I was never the "BRILLIANT CHILD" that teachers praised or relatives spoke proudly about. I passed my Class 10 exams with 57.57%. It was the kind of result that no one celebrated, but at least the neighbours didn't call to console my parents. I wasn't bad; I just wasn't "SPECIAL." And that's how Commerce entered my life—not as a passionate choice, but as the safest seat left in the theatre of Indian education. Commerce was that middle seat on a bus—not uncomfortable, not exciting, just… available. But surprisingly, something changed in 11th and 12th. I found a strange connection with one subject, Accountancy. The debit-credit world made sense to me in a way algebra never did. For the first time, I understood what I was studying, and even more shockingly, I enjoyed it. Yes, I know—'enjoying' a subject in college sounds illegal, but it happened. By the time I reached B.Com, the guy who once got 57% in Class 10 was now in the top 5 students of his college. It was like Sachin Tendulkar getting picked last for gully cricket and then hitting sixes on every ball. Even I was confused: 'Is it me?'

While pursuing **M.Com** through correspondence, I started thinking about my future. Like every obedient student of the Indian education system, I followed the golden formula: study hard, graduate, get a job, and live happily ever after—preferably with Saturday-Sunday off and a DIWALI BONUS. This was the only plan we were shown. The system didn't force us into jobs; it trained us to believe that job was the only destination worth reaching.

And so, I got one.

I joined a recruitment agency at Nariman Point and earned ₹1500-2000 a month. Not bad for a fresher. Later, I got another job in Andheri, and the salary rose to ₹3500-4000. Now I could afford a samosa with my cutting chai and even offer vada pav to a friend on good days. Let me be honest—this isn't one of those dramatic poverty stories. I wasn't starving. I had food at home, and my mother made sure I was never hungry, even if I didn't know what I was doing with my life. But something else was missing: peace. Every day, I woke up early, ran behind trains, got squashed between elbows and backpacks in crowded locals, and travelled over two hours just to reach an office where my chair had more value than my ideas. It was a routine I didn't hate, but I also didn't want to live with it forever.

And then came the moment.

Somewhere between Vasai and Andheri, stuck near the door of a packed train, a thought struck me harder than a station pole: ***"Why am I doing this for ₹4000? If I teach just 20 students for ₹200 per month each, I can make the same money—without hanging from a train like Spider-Man in formals."***

Now here's the funny part.

My brother had already started coaching classes. They were running well. He had gone to Dubai, and teachers here were managing the batches. The entire setup was ready. Like a parked scooter with keys already in the ignition. And I had ignored it completely. Why? Because the system had drilled one thought into my head: *"Earn your own salary."* So I left the running scooter and decided to walk, uphill, barefoot. But that day, in the train, something changed. I realized that instead of dragging myself to an office that barely cared whether I showed up or not, I could take charge of something that was already mine to grow. So I took over the classes. I started teaching myself. I began managing batches, talking to students, building systems, improving quality. I even started freelancing as a visiting faculty in other institutes. Slowly, the classroom became my world, and teaching became my identity. I didn't plan this life. It just happened. But when it did, it felt right. Looking back, I don't blame the system for not making me an entrepreneur. But I do question why it never gave me a hint that I could be one. We studied Business Studies, but no one told us to start a business. We were taught the features of entrepreneurs, but never how to become one. We read about innovation, but never practiced it. We were trained to follow rules, but never to create our own path. Commerce gave us books, batches, and balance sheets, but it didn't give us belief. That belief, I found outside the classroom in crowded trains, in tired evenings, and in the decision to trust myself just a little more. This book isn't about my story. My story is just a small chapter in a bigger picture. This book is about every student who took up Commerce without knowing what they really wanted, every graduate who stepped out of college with a degree but no direction, and every young mind who's still waiting for someone to say, *"You can build your own road."* So if you've ever sat in a train and wondered, *"Is this it?"*, then no, this is not it. You don't need to be born a businessman. You just need one reason to stop being everyone else's employee. And if Commerce is really about business, then it's high time we start teaching how to create one, not just audit one.

But I wasn't the only one who took time to realize his worth. While my story took a turn inside a crowded train, there was another story unfolding quietly, right beside me. A different kind of student, smarter than me, more consistent, and always ahead in class. But just like me, even he never really got to hear those five life-changing words: *"You can do much more."* His story may sound very different, but the ending feels strangely familiar. Let me tell you about him.

The Student Who Never Knew His Own Weight

What if I told you that the student everyone believed would become a successful corporate leader ended up managing a grocery store, not because he lacked ability, but because no one ever showed him there were other possibilities? I had a friend in college who was the complete opposite of me when it came to academics. While I was proudly waving my 57.57% Class 10 result like it was a national flag, he quietly scored over 70%, without breaking a sweat. In 11th and 12th, he was a magician in accountancy. Teachers trusted his answers more than the textbooks. If you ever forgot a concept, his notebook was your savior. While I struggled to remember if debit went left or right, he was preparing to manage the whole ledger. We studied together through FYBCom, SYBCom, and TYBCom. I did enough to stay afloat, but he sailed through. Everyone predicted a bright future for him. People said he would be a financial analyst, a bank officer, maybe even a chartered accountant. Some joked that he was born to become a CEO, and honestly, it wasn't a joke; it felt real. But something unexpected happened after graduation. Instead of going for campus placements or building a corporate career, he simply returned to his father's grocery store. No resumes, no job applications, no HR interviews. Just one quiet decision, to sit at the same counter he had grown up watching. At first, I was stunned. I couldn't believe that a student so talented, so full of potential, had chosen what looked like a very ordinary life. But slowly, I realized something that changed my perspective. While we were spending our evenings in canteens and wasting time talking about some funny stories, he had been building something else entirely. After lectures, he would go directly to the shop and spend two to three hours there every day, dealing with customers, checking stock, managing accounts, and learning the practical side of business without making a big deal about it. During Diwali vacations, while we were watching fireworks, he was selling them. Every year, he set up a firecracker stall in front of his shop and earned more in ten days than many of us earned in a month. This wasn't a backup plan. It was his reality. He didn't just inherit a family business; he embraced it. While the rest of us were learning business theory, he was living it. And the more I thought about it, the more I understood that he had made a conscious choice. He knew that even with the best degree, a high-paying job might not match what he could earn from the shop. More importantly, he was confident in what he was doing. He had clarity. He had vision. He had instinct. And he had something most commerce students don't get: early exposure.

But here's the real question.

Why didn't the education system show him more than one path? Why did it allow such a bright student to continue on the road he was already on, without offering an alternative? Why wasn't he challenged to scale his family business into a chain? Why didn't anyone tell him he could take it online, create a brand, build something beyond the neighbourhood? The system never showed him that he could be more, not because it didn't want to, but because it simply isn't designed to. Commerce education teaches us how to record profit, but not how to create it. It teaches us about business laws, but not how to break barriers. It prepares us for employment, not for enterprise. And so, a student who had the ability to become a CEO ended up behind a grocery counter. Not by failure, but by default. Not because he lacked skill, but because the system lacked vision. He never got to ask himself, *"What else can I be?"* because no one around him ever asked that question either. That's when I realized, we are producing intelligent students with powerful minds, but limited awareness. Like an elephant that doesn't know how heavy it is, they carry great potential, but live with small ambition. They don't know what they're capable of, so they settle for whatever path is visible.

And that's the real tragedy.

Because education is not just about finishing chapters and passing exams. It's about opening minds, showing roads, and creating belief. A student should walk out of college thinking, *"Yes, I can be a great employee, but I can also build something of my own. I have that option. I have that power."* But most of them never think this way, because the system never taught them to. My friend chose the path he was raised with. And he's doing well. But maybe, just maybe, if someone had shown him the second road, he would have built something that went far beyond his father's shop. He could have built history. Education can only succeed when it shows students who they are, and what they can become. Because the saddest thing isn't when a student fails. It's when a student never finds out how far he could have gone.

But not every student avoids entrepreneurship because of a lack of exposure. Some avoid it because they've seen too much. While one student quietly embraced his father's grocery shop, another ran away from his father's business — not because he didn't understand it, but because he understood it too well. His fear didn't come from failure — it came from observation. Let me tell you about him.

The Burden of Observation — The Boy Who Feared His Father's Business

"Sir, I don't want to end up like my father."

That sentence hit me like a thunderbolt.

I had simply asked one of my brightest students if he ever thought about taking over his father's successful wholesale business. He looked down, paused, and said with a calm but serious face, *"I've seen his life. Early mornings, late nights, customers chasing payments, suppliers calling non-stop. He built a great business, but at what cost? I don't want to live like that. I want peace. I want weekends. I want a job that ends at 5 PM."* At first, I smiled. I thought he was joking. But he wasn't. This boy, who could explain business models better than the textbook, who scored top marks in entrepreneurship papers, who could easily run his father's empire with a modern twist — had no interest in business.

Why? Because to him, entrepreneurship didn't look like freedom. It looked like fatigue. His entire understanding of business came not from what was taught in the classroom — but from what he saw at home. And what he saw wasn't a boss living his dream. What he saw was a man who looked ten years older than his age. He told me, *"Sir, some days my father would be searching the whole house for ₹100, like he lost a treasure. And other days, he would pull out ₹10,000 from a file that no one knew existed. We never knew whether to celebrate or to worry."* The boy laughed and continued, *"Sometimes, my dad would suddenly decide we're buying a four-wheeler. 'Let's go book it!' he'd say with full confidence. And just when we'd start feeling like royalty, two months later — boom! — he'd sell the car because cash was stuck in the market."* He gave one more classic example: *"Once, my mom got a beautiful gold necklace out of nowhere. She was showing it to everyone like a trophy. Three weeks later, that same necklace went straight back to the jeweller during a crisis."* He looked at me and said, *"Sir, I'm not afraid of hard work. I'm afraid of instability. I'm not afraid of customers. I'm afraid of that moment when my father sits at the edge of the bed, silent, staring at the ceiling, because some payment didn't come through."* And honestly, I couldn't argue with him. Because while we teach students the features of sole proprietorship, we forget to teach them how to manage it with peace of mind. While we ask them to memorize "FUNCTIONS OF A MANAGER," we never train them to become one inside their own homes. To him, business meant being alert 24/7, no off days, no holidays, no peace. It was not inspiration. It was irritation. It was not a dream. It was pressure wrapped in paperwork. But here's where education missed a big opportunity.

If Commerce education had shown him how to manage finances better, how to automate tasks, how to bring structure and systems into his father's business — maybe he would've believed he could do it differently. Maybe he wouldn't run from the business. Maybe he would rebuild it with balance. What if education had helped him see that he could turn his father's tension into a company's transformation? What if someone had taught him that today's business doesn't have to look like yesterday's burden? What if someone told him that with modern tools and fresh thinking, he could make that same business smart, scalable, and stress-free? But we didn't. We taught him what a business is. We didn't teach him what a business could be. And so, he turned away. He chose the safer road — employment. Fixed hours. Stable salary. No tension. No customers calling on a Sunday. Just peace and a punch card. And that's the real loss. Because Commerce education, instead of rebuilding a broken student's confidence, often just tells him to avoid the crack and walk on the safe sidewalk. When a student who has seen business chaos at home comes to college hoping for answers — and all he gets are definitions — how can we expect him to dream of entrepreneurship?

And then, there are some students — especially girls — who aren't running away from business or confused about careers. They're not even allowed to think that far. Because in their world, a commerce degree isn't about building a career… it's about building a better marriage proposal. From grocery shops to wedding shops, the journey of commerce takes another unexpected turn.

Commerce for Dowry or Destiny?

A Degree with a Mangalsutra Attached

"Sir, once I become a graduate, my father says I'll get a better marriage proposal."

She said it with the calmness of someone reading a bus timetable. No excitement. No confusion. Just certainty. To her, B.Com wasn't about becoming something. It was about being presentable on the marriage market. That day I realized something important. Commerce, which was created to teach balance sheets, budgeting, and business building, was now being used by some families as a certificate of culture and good behavior. In these homes, education is not for building dreams—it's for building dowry value. And the most tragic part? No one thinks there's anything wrong with it. She wasn't alone. Over the years, I've met many such girls. Bright, capable, and even ambitious deep inside, but surrounded by a family and a system that never allowed them to explore life beyond the kitchen or a wedding stage. Commerce wasn't chosen with purpose. It was chosen because science had too many books, arts were considered *"an Unwanted Degree,"* by some families and commerce... well, commerce looked safe and "SHAADI-APPROPRIATE."

Her parents didn't care about entrepreneurship, finance, or digital marketing. They only cared that the degree would help her find a well-settled boy who worked in an office, preferably one who drove a two-wheeler and had an LIC policy. *"Graduate girls get better boys"* — that was the logic. A B.Com degree wasn't her ticket to independence. It was her ticket to a better groom. I remember asking her softly, *"Don't you want to work?"* She smiled politely and said, *"If my husband allows me, maybe part-time."* And just like that, her dreams had a clause. *"Terms and conditions apply."*

Her family didn't want her to top the university. They just wanted her to top someone's guest list. She wasn't here for campus placements — she was here to make sure she was "MARRIAGE-READY" by 22. It was painful and funny at the same time. Imagine teaching someone how to calculate return on investment when she knows she'll never be allowed to invest. Imagine teaching someone entrepreneurship, when her startup plan begins and ends with *"what's cooking for dinner?"* Commerce had become a waiting room. A three-year gap between HSC results and wedding bells. These students attended classes, gave exams, and filled forms — but they were not filling dreams. They were just filling time. This isn't a small issue. It's a mindset problem. A deep-rooted one. And our education system, knowingly or unknowingly, is supporting it. We talk about women's empowerment in seminars, but in classrooms, many girls are just waiting to be handed over — degree in one hand, suitcase in the other.

As author Chimamanda Ngozi Adichie once said,

"We teach girls to shrink themselves, to make themselves smaller."

"We say to girls: You can have ambition, but not too much."

That's exactly what's happening here. These girls could become brilliant marketers, entrepreneurs, or brand-builders. But before they even get the chance, they are made to believe that their final project is not a business pitch—it's a wedding. And to be honest, sometimes I wonder, should we just make a new subject for them?

"TYBCom Specialization in Marriage Management"

Assignments:

How to manage relatives during functions

Monthly budget planning for groceries

Presentation skills for first tea meeting with in-laws

We laugh, yes. But it's not really funny. Because when education becomes a background decoration in a wedding photo, it loses its real value. Commerce is supposed to give confidence, not just certificates. It should be a platform to build self-worth, not just matrimonial worth. When we say *"empowerment through education,"* it must go beyond posters and slogans. It must reflect in the mindset. It must reflect in the freedom. And most importantly, it must reflect over time.

And then, there are students who aren't waiting for marriage they're waiting for a salary. For some, the degree is not a bridal ticket but a monthly income passport. If one story is about dreams locked in a suitcase, the next is about dreams stuck in a salary slip. From shaadi-ready to salary-ready, commerce continues to be misunderstood. But in both cases, one thing is missing: the courage to create.

The Monthly Salary Mindset

All Business on Paper. No Business in Practice.

"Sir, my father says I must get a job after graduation. I need to earn a fixed income and support the family." He didn't say it with passion. He didn't say it with panic. He said it with the same energy people use to order a plain dosa—no masala, no butter, just basic survival. And he's not alone.

Most commerce students today walk into college with a fully downloaded mindset: *"Get the degree. Get the job. Get out."* Which is ironic—because this is commerce. The stream that's supposed to build CEOs, founders, freelancers, creators—not just *"fresher resumes available on request"*.

Let's be honest—our commerce classrooms are like diet samosas.

They look heavy from the outside, but there's nothing spicy inside.

We teach students the definition of "ENTREPRENEURSHIP,"

but we never teach them how to think like an ENTREPRENEUR.

We make them write 2,000 words on Steve Jobs,

but we never ask them to sell even one actual product.

One student proudly told me, *"Sir, I made a beautiful PPT on how Ola disrupted the transport industry."* I asked, *"Have you ever tried selling one ride pass or even made an app logo?"* He said, *"No Sir, but I got full marks in viva."* That's the problem. We've turned commerce education into a theory museum.

Students visit, observe, memorize, and exit. They know how to prepare final accounts for a fake company in a textbook, but they have no idea how to handle a real customer with real feedback. They've learned everything except how to make money, lose money, recover money, and most importantly, risk money. Our classes have subjects with powerful names: Business Law, Marketing Management, Leadership Skills, but the only law most students follow is: "Get attendance. Pass exam. Forget everything."

Let's be brutally honest: We're not teaching commerce. We're teaching how to become better clerks, assistants, and followers just with fancier job titles and Canva resumes. One of my students said, *"Sir, I want to join a multinational company."* I said, *"Great! What kind of work excites you?"* He replied, *"Whatever they give, as long as there's a good canteen and second Saturday off."* This is where we are. We've created a system where students are trained to calculate someone else's profit, but are never encouraged to create their own. And we wonder why only 2% of commerce graduates become entrepreneurs?

It's because our education system hands out books, but not belief.

It teaches accounts, but not accountability for dreams.

It teaches theory of business, but never the thrill of business.

Commerce should be the most exciting stream — it's about money, marketing, and making moves. But instead, we've made it feel like an endless queue at the bank: Too slow, too dull, and full of forms. But here's the good news: This can change. Add real business projects. Let students sell, pitch, and fail, and try again. Bring in street-smart entrepreneurs, not just retired bankers in guest lectures. Make internships mandatory — not just as a box to tick, but as a real experience. Because if we keep feeding students theory and fear, we'll keep producing more *"job-seekers with degrees"* and fewer *"visionaries with ideas."* Commerce education has the content. Now it needs some courage. And a lot more masala.

Only then will a commerce student say:

"Sir, I'm not waiting for a job.
I'm ready to create one."

And just when you think the only problem is students chasing jobs, another twist walks in — students who don't want jobs at all. No interviews, no resumes, no LinkedIn. Just one goal: *"Sit at the family shop and continue the legacy."* One side is afraid of freedom, the other is allergic to structure. Somewhere between salary slips and stubborn family businesses, education stands confused, wondering, *"Am I even needed here?"*

When Family Says "ONLY BUSINESS," and Education Just Watches

He was one of those students every teacher remembers. Bright, fluent, sharp, and confident. The kind of boy who could stand up in class and speak like a future CEO. I often thought to myself, *"This one will go far."* Years later, after graduation, I saw him again. Not in a boardroom, not in a corporate office — but behind the counter of a small mobile shop. He stood there smiling, relaxed, greeting customers as if he owned the world. I walked up to him, surprised, and asked, *"Why this? I thought you were aiming for a big company job."*

He looked at me with calm eyes and said, *"Sir, in my family we are taught only one thing: do business. Even if you earn less, earn with dignity and independence."* That one line stayed with me. It struck more deeply than any lecture I had ever given. His degree had given him knowledge, but his family had already written his future. And between the two, it was the family that won.

Back in college, I understood why he behaved the way he did. He never really came to explore commerce. He came only to confirm what he already believed that jobs are for others, not for him. In his mind, working under someone was a failure. Asking him to consider a corporate job was like asking a lion to wear a necktie.

When I taught business law, he asked me if it would help renew his shop license.

When I explained marketing strategies, he wanted only tips about hoarding rates.

When I spoke of leadership, he would quietly say, *"Sir, my dad already runs the shop his way."*

This wasn't learning. This was filtering. From the entire ocean of commerce education, he only collected one bucket of water—the one that matched his family's script. And yet, he was brilliant. That's what pained me the most. He had the spark to be a great manager, a leader, maybe even a visionary CEO. But his path was already closed before it began. His family's voice was louder than his own ambition. I once encouraged him to participate in a startup pitching competition. He smiled and said, *"Sir, I already have a startup. My father started it in 1998."* *I replied, "Then at least bring something new to it." But he shook his head, "Sir, my father says don't fix what's not broken."*

And with that, innovation quietly died in my classroom. That day I realized something important: we often blame education for producing jobseekers, but what about families that reject jobs completely? What about students who are told from day one, *"You are born only to run our shop"?*

The irony is, these same families proudly display the degree like a showroom board: *"Look, our son is a graduate. He is educated."* But behind that board, the boy is trapped at the family counter, never allowed to think beyond it. And here's the bitter truth: no matter how hard a teacher tries, education cannot help a student who isn't open to being helped. It's like joining a cooking class only to learn how to boil water.

This isn't just one boy's story. It's a mindset crisis. A boundary set by families, sealed in the name of dignity, while education quietly watches from the back row—taking attendance, collecting files, but never strong enough to shake the blueprint.

Not every student walks into college with an open mind. Some walk in with a closed book, already written by their parents. Until education becomes bold enough to challenge those pages, we will keep losing brilliant minds—not to failure, but to narrow vision.

As author Alvin Toffler once said:

"The illiterate of the 21st century will not be those who cannot read and write,but those who cannot learn, unlearn, and relearn."

But how will students unlearn, if their families have already written the ending of the story? Commerce education must do more than just teach chapters. It must challenge comfort zones. It must not just give information—it must give permission. Permission to think, to explore, to step beyond the shop shutter and dream something of their own. Because if we keep producing students who attend college just to earn family approval, not personal growth, we are not educating them. We're just rubber-stamping their destiny—and proudly calling it a degree.

After reading all these real-life stories, you might be wondering—who's actually at fault here? Is it the student who never looked inside to discover his real strength? The parent who decided the career path based on the family WhatsApp group? The education system that hands out degrees like discount coupons? The teacher who never saw the spark in the backbenchers? Or the college that's more focused on cultural programs than career counselling? Frankly… it's like asking, *"Who put too much salt in the biryani?"* when the rice is already half-cooked, the chicken is missing, and no one even turned on the stove. We started with the story of an Unexpected Entrepreneur—a student who became a coaching class owner by accident, and then realised, *"Why didn't college teach me this was possible?"* Then we met another boy—smart, confident, ready to manage a business but mentally locked into a job mindset like a computer stuck on **Ctrl+Alt+Salary.** Then came the reverse situation—a student with real manager material, but trapped in a family that said, **"Forget the degree, handle the shop."** We met girls who treated B.Com like a pre-wedding course. We met students living under the monthly salary mindset, where dreams are replaced by survival plans. And finally, we saw a student who came to college not to learn, but to confirm what his family already decided—*"Business is the only way."* Every story gave us a different villain. Sometimes it was fear. Sometimes it was tradition. Sometimes it was the syllabus. And sometimes… it was the Wi-Fi speed in college—because when you have no access to opportunity, even Google can't guide your future. And while some students are locked inside family businesses they never questioned, others are gently pulled away from dreams they once believed in. Not by pressure, but by practicality. Not by force, but by affection. Some never got the freedom to choose… others were given the freedom, but with invisible strings attached. What looks like "ADJUSTMENT" from the outside is often just a silent goodbye to a passion that couldn't survive the wait. And that brings us to the next story—where a dream didn't die in a day… it simply faded, step by step.

When Dreams Are Silently Rewritten

It was a quiet evening when a father decided to take his son on a long bike ride. The CLASS 10 results had just come out, and he thought a little fresh air and an open road would help open up a bigger conversation—one that every parent eventually has with their child: **"What next?"** Now, this wasn't a controlling father. In fact, he was supportive, gentle, and modern in his outlook. He had only one rule—whatever his son decides, he would stand by it. The son had been holding back his feelings, but that one assurance gave him the courage he needed. He turned to his father, and with a voice full of emotion said, *"Dad, I want to do something different. Something creative. I want to become a film director."* The father didn't say anything immediately. He just kept riding. On the outside, he looked calm. But on the inside, a hundred questions had already begun to spin in his mind. *"Director? Film industry? Creativity?"* These words were foreign to his practical, middle-class upbringing. His heart said, *"Let him follow his dream,"* but his mind said, *"What if it doesn't work out?"* He wanted to protect his son, not discourage him. So instead of reacting, he simply said, *"Beta, give me two days to think about this. Let's talk again."* Those two days were difficult. The father spoke to his friends, his family, and even had long moments of silent reflection. He thought about the world his son wanted to enter—the chaos of the film industry, the uncertainty, the fierce competition. His son had never shown a deep interest in drama, never participated in stage plays or directed school events. Was this dream genuine? Or was it just a passing phase triggered by watching too many movies? Still, he didn't want to be the villain in his child's story. He knew that even if he disagreed, his son's trust in him mattered more than any decision. And so, he searched for a balanced solution.

When they met again for another ride, the father had a plan. He said, *"Beta, if you really want to be a director, I'm not stopping you. There's a film institute 200 kilometers from here. It's a good one. But right now, you're too young to live alone so far from home. I won't feel comfortable sending you away just after your Class 10. So here's what I propose: you take up commerce for two years, stay close to home, and after your HSC, I'll personally get you admitted to that film institute. No questions asked."* It sounded fair. The son, still high on his dream, agreed. After all, it was just two years. He'd pass the time, do commerce, and then jump into his real passion. Or so he thought. Those two years did what two years always do—they changed things. New friends, new teachers, new ways of thinking. Slowly, his dream of becoming a film director faded not because he stopped loving it, but because he started adapting to the world around him. He wasn't pushed. He wasn't forced. But the environment gently nudged him in a different direction. When his HSC results came, his father took him out again for another career talk. This time, things were different. The boy looked calm, more mature. He said, *"Dad, I don't think I want to be a director anymore. I want to study computers. I want to do BCA."* The father smiled—not because he had won—but because he felt his son had chosen something practical, something stable. He immediately got him enrolled in a Bachelor of Computer Applications course. Everyone was happy. Problem solved. Or was it?

Let's pause here.

Was this really his decision? Or had time and environment made the decision for him? Was he adjusting? Or was he growing? It's a fine line. Sometimes, children don't give up on their dreams because they want to. They give up because they no longer recognize their dream in the mirror. And when a new path is shown to them—especially one that's more socially acceptable, easier to explain to relatives, and more secure—they slowly start walking on it. And after a while, they convince themselves it was their own choice. This story is not just about one boy. It's the story of thousands of students who dream of becoming actors, photographers, pilots, chefs, or artists—but end up in commerce, not out of love, but out of adjustment. They're told, *"Take commerce for now. You can always switch later."* But sometimes, later never comes. And the dream that once lit their eyes becomes just a memory they smile at and say, *"That's what I wanted once."* Commerce isn't the villain here. But we must admit—many students don't choose commerce because they're passionate about economics or accountancy. They choose it because it's safe, affordable, and familiar. Very few students walk into a commerce classroom saying, *"This is exactly what I've always wanted to do."* Most treat it as a stepping stone, a waiting area, a PLAN B. And that's the tragedy. Commerce, as a stream, is often reduced to a backup plan. And dreams? They quietly take the backseat. The boy in our story had the heart of a director. But two years of passive influence, peer conversations, and indirect pressure reshaped him into a computer student. He might succeed. He might even love his new field. But the world may have lost a passionate filmmaker.

To every parent reading this, this is not an accusation. It's a gentle reminder. When your child speaks about becoming something wild, something big, something uncertain—pause. Don't immediately look for the nearest "safe" alternative. Don't sell them an adjustment in the name of maturity. Listen. Support. Believe. Because sometimes, all a child needs is not a **BETTER COURSE,** but a **BRAVER PARENT.**

And just when you think dreams only fade in the world of glamour and film, meet another boy one who didn't want to become a filmmaker, engineer, or millionaire. He just wanted a peaceful life on three wheels. No red carpets, no boardrooms, just a rickshaw and the open road. One dream came with lights and cameras. The other with simplicity and silence. But both tell the same truth when decisions are delayed, dreams quietly adjust. And sometimes, they disappear without a fight. Let's see what happened when simplicity met society.

When Simplicity Meets Society

It was a regular evening in a small chawl where dreams were often measured by how practical they sounded. A father sat in the corner of his room, sipping tea, when his son came and quietly sat next to him. The boy was in Class 10, barely managing to pass his subjects, and clearly not excited by the idea of textbooks, exams, or results. There was always a sense of discomfort when it came to studies. That evening, something inside the boy gave him the courage to speak openly. And what he said caught his father completely off guard. "ABBU," he began, *"I don't want to study anymore. Please don't force me. I want to drive a rickshaw. I like that life. Rickshaw drivers are free they go where they want, they stop when they want. No pressure, no boss, no stress. Just me and the road. Please get me a rickshaw."* The father didn't react immediately. He simply looked at his son's face. The boy wasn't joking. His eyes were serious. In his heart, the idea of driving a rickshaw felt like peace, freedom, and a way to avoid the struggle of education he never connected with. The father felt a strange mix of emotions shock, sadness, and confusion. Should he scold him? Should he crush his dream? Or should he try to understand where this was coming from? But instead of saying no directly, the father chose a smarter route. He smiled and said, *"Beta, I'm not saying no. But to get a rickshaw license, you need to be eighteen. You're still young. Till then, just continue your studies. When you turn eighteen, I promise I'll get you a rickshaw if you still want it."* The boy nodded. It felt like a fair deal. He agreed. For the next two years, he enrolled in the commerce stream. Not because he loved accounts or economics, but because it was a temporary plan, a waiting room until his "REAL LIFE" could begin.

But just like in the earlier story of the boy who once wanted to become a director, time worked its quiet magic again. Two years of being around commerce students, attending lectures, discussing subjects, and getting used to a structured environment slowly brought about a shift in the boy's mind. He saw that commerce offered many options: B.Com, BAF, BMS, diplomas, certifications. There was variety. There was direction. And most importantly, there was dignity. The dream of the rickshaw began to fade not because someone killed it, but because the boy himself started seeing life differently. The idea of wandering the streets freely was replaced by thoughts of doing something more stable, more "RESPECTABLE." Even if he wasn't going to be a doctor or engineer, at least he wouldn't be someone the world looked down upon.

And this is where the real question begins. If we say every child must follow their passion, should we have allowed this boy to follow his and become a rickshaw driver? Is passion valid only when it leads to a glamorous profession like film direction or fashion design? What about a child who wants a simple life? Who finds joy in average living? Most parents reading this will agree with the father's decision. *"Of course, he should be guided. You can't let a child throw his life away."* But then, doesn't that contradict the idea of letting a child follow his dream? Just because a dream doesn't sound impressive or ambitious doesn't mean it's not real. Some children genuinely feel happy doing basic things. Not every child wants to become rich or famous. Some enjoy simplicity. And sometimes, they are the most peaceful ones in society. But family pressure, social image, and the fear of "WHAT WILL PEOPLE SAY" drive parents to save their child's future even if it means redirecting or delaying their choices. In doing so, many parents gently nudge their children into commerce, not because the child loves it, but because it's the safest ship to board when the sea of life feels confusing.

And slowly, over the years, the value of commerce as a stream starts to fall. It becomes the home for confused students, not passionate ones. Those who can't decide, or those who are avoiding something, quietly take refuge in the world of commerce. It becomes the backup plan, the shelter, the compromise. And that's where the deeper issue lies. Commerce isn't just about accounts and economics.

It's supposed to be about understanding the real business world. But when the majority of students enter it as a last resort, without purpose or vision, the quality of learning goes down. The seriousness goes down. And in the end, the stream that once built traders, entrepreneurs, and professionals becomes a dumping ground for directionless students.

The real issue is not that the child wanted to become a rickshaw driver. The issue is that he was pushed into commerce without any real interest in it. And when thousands of students like him enter commerce as an escape, not a choice, the stream starts losing its value. Commerce becomes a home for lost dreams, not built visions. And in that process, both the student and the subject suffer quietly.

And just when you think dreams only get redirected towards something "RESPECTABLE," comes the story of a boy whose heart didn't beat for studies or even simplicity; it beat for cricket. Not for comfort, not for fame, just pure love for the game. One boy wanted peace on a rickshaw. This one wanted pride on the pitch. But both were passengers on the same train called "COMMERCE," not because they chose it, but because someone else booked the ticket. Let's meet a young cricketer who didn't fail in life life simply didn't field him at the right position.

Got Caught in Commerce

He wasn't born with books in his hand. He was born with a bat in his grip and dreams in his eyes. From a very young age, this boy was drawn to cricket. He wasn't just playing it—he was living it. He played for his school team, joined local coaching clubs, and was even selected for seasonal cricket tournaments. For him, cricket wasn't just a game; it was a calling. Cricket ran through his veins the way rhythm flows through a musician or paint through an artist's brush. Everyone around him knew—this boy was made for cricket. But then came the harsh truth of his world. He belonged to a middle-class family—a family that believed in safe paths, stable jobs, and familiar roads. For them, cricket was just a hobby. A pastime. Not a career. The word "PROFESSIONAL" was never attached to sports. In their eyes, cricket was something you watched on TV, not something you invested your life into. And so, like many dreams in Indian households, his too was gently folded, kept in a drawer, and replaced with something "SAFER"—commerce.

He joined a nearby college. Not because he loved business studies or wanted to become a CA or MBA. He joined because his passion had no place in his parents' rulebook. Even in college, the spark didn't die. He still played cricket. He still found time to practice—sometimes early mornings, sometimes late evenings. No matter how tired he was, or how long the lectures were, cricket always found space in his schedule. He wasn't an extraordinary national-level player, not yet. But what he had was rare—unshakable passion. Now here's where the system failed him again. Since his marks were average and there was no vacancy under sports quota, he didn't get admission to a reputed college that supported athletics. So he ended up in a regular commerce college—one with no proper cricket ground, no good coaches, and no active sports department. What was he supposed to do? A cricket lover, trapped in a classroom that didn't even acknowledge his talent. So again, we must ask: Whose fault was it? Was it the system that measures a player's worth by their percentage instead of their potential? Was it the college that didn't provide basic sports infrastructure? Was it the parents who failed to trust their child's instincts? Or was it the student, who didn't fight hard enough? Maybe he wasn't the next Virat Kohli. But he was someone who breathed cricket. And passion, when given the right direction, turns into performance. The fire was there. But no one brought the spark to life. Slowly, he started adjusting. The bat was replaced by books. The match schedules were replaced by exam timetables. And the dream? It was never killed. It just got tired of waiting. There are hundreds of students like him. They want to become athletes, artists, dancers, gamers, filmmakers, but they are put into commerce like it's a lifeboat. And when they step into that lifeboat, their dream starts sinking slowly.

So the question is: are these students going to strengthen the value of commerce? Or are they going to weaken it? When students enter commerce not because they want to, but because they have no other choice, what happens to the purpose of this stream? Commerce then stops being a space for builders and creators. It becomes a shelter for compromised dreams. This isn't just one story. This is a mirror. A mirror that reflects every parent who changed their child's direction "FOR THEIR GOOD," every college that didn't build support systems for non-academic talents, and every system that values numbers over passion.

We say "FOLLOW YOUR PASSION." But what if a child's passion doesn't fit in your degree chart? What if it doesn't promise a stable salary? What if it looks risky? Should we still support it?

The answer is **YES.**

Because if we don't, we're not just changing careers — we are replacing original dreams with borrowed plans. And then, even when students succeed on paper, their soul quietly stays unsatisfied. Let us stop building careers on fear and pressure. Let us start building them on purpose and belief. Because not every child is meant to sit in front of a computer. Some are meant to run on a cricket pitch.

And when passion slowly fades, what replaces it? Reality. Harsh, honest, unavoidable reality. The cricket bat goes into the cupboard, the canvas remains blank, and the camera gathers dust… and in its place, enters the offer letter with a starting salary that barely covers rent. This next story isn't about what a student wanted to become. It's about what life allowed him to become. Because after years of studying finance, most commerce graduates aren't managing investments — they're managing survival. Let's now meet a young man who, like many, got a degree… but not the financial life it promised.

The Salary Trap: A Story of Survival, Not Growth

There is one more question that often troubles my mind. What does a commerce student really earn after completing his degree? Whether it's B.Com, BAF, or BMS, after spending three years in college, what salary does the industry offer to a fresh commerce graduate?

Let's look at the reality.

By the time a student completes his graduation, he is around 20 to 22 years old. After all the years of schooling, junior college, and degree education, now comes the moment when both the student and the family expect some return. In most middle-class and lower-middle-class families, parents wait for their child to complete graduation so that he can start earning and support the family. But sadly, for many commerce graduates, the starting salary is just enough for survival. Forget about savings. Forget about investments. Forget about wealth creation. The monthly income they receive barely helps them run the house. Financial literacy, economic awareness, investment planning, these are all beautiful words that remain trapped inside textbooks.

In reality, financial planning starts only when a person has extra money after fulfilling his basic needs. But when the salary itself is too small, how can one think of investments or wealth management? Most of the income simply goes into daily expenses—house rent, food, transportation, and helping parents and siblings. This is the bitter truth for 50-60% of India's middle-class and lower-middle-class commerce graduates. They don't start their professional life with dreams of becoming investors or entrepreneurs. They start with one simple goal—survival.

As time passes and their salaries slightly increase, new responsibilities arise: marriage, children, house, and loans. Soon they find themselves trapped in a vicious cycle of EMIs, debts, and never-ending expenses. At the stage when they could have thought about wealth creation, another alarm rings:

"Now you need to settle down and buy a house."

To buy a house, they take heavy loans. And once the loan starts, the game of financial stress begins—month after month, year after year. By then, all the beautiful theories of financial literacy and economic awareness that they read during their commerce education remain only in books—never applied in their real lives. Here again, I am not talking about the few lucky ones who manage to break this cycle. I am talking about the large number of students—the masses—for whom commerce education did not give enough tools to fight this financial struggle.

Commerce education teaches about finance, but life demands survival first.

A Missing Lesson in Commerce Education

As we move ahead in this book, we have already seen how commerce education struggles to build entrepreneurs and creators. But there is one more silent weakness that often stays hidden behind degrees and certificates. It is the fear to stand and speak in front of others—the fear to face a crowd. This stage fear has become one of the most common problems among commerce students. They study for years, they pass examinations, they collect degrees, but when they are asked to stand in front of just ten people and speak, their hands start shaking, their voice becomes weak, and their mind goes blank. This fear becomes a silent barrier that holds them back from expressing their thoughts confidently.

Surprisingly, these same students, after five or six years of working in a job, start leading meetings, talking to clients, giving presentations, and even training others. The question is simple—if they can develop these skills after graduation in the real world, why can't our education system train them during graduation itself? Why should industry alone be responsible for giving them this confidence? Why can't our colleges give them this strength while they are still students?

Commerce education today focuses on books, theory, and exams. Students memorize definitions, write answers, and score marks. But when it comes to presenting their knowledge or speaking in front of an audience, they hesitate. A small group of students, who naturally love to participate in college events or competitions, manage to overcome this fear early. But the majority of students remain untouched. The education system does not create enough opportunities for every student to face people, express ideas, or learn the art of communication. Speaking is not just about standing on a stage. It is about having the confidence to express one's ideas in meetings, discussions, interviews, and day-to-day professional life. Leadership begins with the courage to speak up. But this lesson is often missing from the classrooms. From my years of teaching, I have observed one truth again and again. Leadership is not a gift given at birth. Every student has the potential to lead if they are guided properly. Just like reading and writing, speaking confidently is a skill that can be taught. But unfortunately, our commerce education rarely provides space for this training. Students are never encouraged to make presentations, participate in debates, or face mock interviews regularly. Marks become more important than expression. Examinations test memory, not courage. In some places, even teachers avoid giving students public speaking tasks because they feel it may waste class time or affect the syllabus. As a result, a large group of commerce graduates graduate every year, but they carry this silent fear with them into the real world. The transformation that happens after graduation is proof that this skill can be developed. Once these students enter jobs, they are forced to speak, lead teams, face clients, and handle meetings. Slowly, they start learning how to express their thoughts. They gain confidence through experience, trial, and error. The industry teaches them what the college should have taught long before. If this confidence can be built later, it means it can also be built earlier—within the education system itself.

When we talk about real-life examples, one story that always inspires me is that of Dhirubhai Ambani, the founder of Reliance Industries. Born in a simple family in Chorwad, Gujarat, Dhirubhai did not attend any fancy business school. In fact, during his early years, he had very little formal education. But life became his teacher. He started his career as a petrol station attendant in Yemen. Every day, he interacted with different people, listened to their stories, learned new things, and slowly built his confidence. He never feared speaking to people, whether they were customers or businessmen. His ability to communicate, negotiate, and build relationships became his strongest leadership skill. Over the years, this confidence helped him build one of the biggest business empires in India. Dhirubhai Ambani's story shows that leadership and confidence are not about degrees or marks; they are about exposure, practice, and fearlessness. If education can create such environments of practice within colleges, many students can develop these skills much earlier in life.

Education should not wait for the industry to do its unfinished work. It should prepare students completely before they step into the real world. The classrooms must not only be centers for reading and writing but also stages where students learn to speak, discuss, debate, and present. Every subject should have a space where students are required to present what they have learned. Group discussions, presentations, role plays, and mock interviews should not be optional activities but a part of regular learning. Even shy students must be gently encouraged and trained to face the class. Small leadership roles in classrooms, college events, and academic discussions can build the foundation for future leadership. When a student learns to face people during graduation, he or she becomes far more prepared for professional challenges later. He or she carries confidence not only in knowledge but also in communication. In the world of business, where ideas matter as much as knowledge, the ability to express can make all the difference between a leader and a follower.

John F. Kennedy once said, **"Leadership and learning are indispensable to each other."** If we want our commerce students to become future leaders, we must blend leadership training into the learning process itself. Only then will we not just produce graduates with degrees but young professionals who can walk confidently onto any stage and lead the way.

Teachers often say, *"We give them chances, we make announcements, it's up to the students to come forward."* But is that enough? Shouldn't it be the responsibility of the teachers and the system to bring the shy students out of their shells? Are we only helping the 20% who are already confident, while silently ignoring the 80% who are hiding in the crowd? Leadership, public speaking, and risk-taking are not traits you're born with; they are skills that can be developed, just like writing or mathematics. But most commerce students graduate without ever testing these waters. And the cost of this delay is huge.

I still remember one of my former students. He was extremely shy, afraid to even stand up in class. He never participated in a single event, never went near a stage. A few years later — almost five or six years after college— I met him again. I was shocked. He was speaking fluently in English, confidently leading conversations, and showing the body language of a leader. I was amazed by the transformation. I asked him,

"What changed you?"

He smiled and replied, "Sir, I had no choice. I spent five years in a company where I was forced to speak up, lead meetings, and handle clients. My situation made me strong. My fear had no place there." His words struck me deeply. Why must we wait for the outside world to shape our students? Why can't colleges prepare them during their most important years? Why should fear be broken only by corporate pressure and not classroom preparation? Commerce education must include more than textbooks and exams. It must teach students how to stand up, speak out, and lead with confidence. Group discussions, mock interviews, stage presentations, anchoring, event management —these should not be optional extras but essential experiences. Only then will we create commerce graduates who are not just qualified on paper but equipped to face the world boldly.

The Trap of Free Time - When Career Takes a Backseat

An idle mind is the devil's workshop.

As students enter regular college life, one thing they often find in abundance is free time. Classes are limited to a few hours a day. Assignments and exams come only once in a while. What remains is long stretches of free time that is rarely utilized in a productive way. While a few students take this time seriously, joining part-time jobs, internships, or extra learning courses, a large majority spend these hours in building friendships, hanging out in groups, and slowly entering into personal relationships. At first, it feels harmless—friends sitting together for hours, planning trips, discussing movies, or simply passing time. But slowly, for many, these friendships turn into serious affairs. This is where the real distraction begins. Once serious relationships start, many students begin to shift their focus from career-building to planning their personal lives. Parents, under pressure of society, sometimes start discussing early marriages even before the student completes his or her education. Now, instead of focusing on skill development or future planning, the student's mind gets trapped in emotional attachments and family discussions. Slowly, the student's career takes a backseat, and decisions start revolving around marriage dates, family approval, and financial arrangements. What was once free time for growth now becomes a trap that prevents many students from moving ahead.

I remember a real story from my own teaching experience. There was a bright student (girl), who was pursuing her B.Com degree. She was smart, good at accounts, and had big dreams to pursue higher studies. But during her second year, she got deeply involved in a relationship with one of her classmates. As time passed, both families came to know each other, and soon discussions of marriage started. By the time she reached her final year, her engagement was already fixed. She gave up her plans for further studies because her marriage was scheduled right after graduation. Today, while her batchmates are completing professional courses and building their careers, she is busy managing home responsibilities. I do not say this to criticize anyone's personal choices. But it is a reality that in many cases, free time and early emotional involvement pull students away from their long-term career growth.

The problem here is not friendship or relationships. The problem is the lack of proper guidance and structure during these important years. If the education system can fill this free time with career counseling, leadership training, internships, and skill-based courses, many students will find themselves too busy building their future to fall into these early distractions. As the famous author Napoleon Hill said, *"Idle time is the beginning of all mischief."* The system must give students a meaningful direction before free time becomes their biggest enemy.

In the beginning of my career, like many teachers, I started with junior college teaching commerce to 11th and 12th standard students. It felt like the right place to begin. The syllabus was manageable, the students were young and curious, and I was eager to shape minds. At the same time, I was personally focused on health and fitness. I followed a gym routine and controlled my diet. I believed if I wanted to guide others, I had to keep myself mentally and physically disciplined. About five or six years passed. One evening, I was out with friends, enjoying a regular tea break at a local tapri, a place where people casually gather to sip chai and chat. As we stood talking, I noticed a thin, short man repeatedly looking at me. At first, I ignored it, but his eyes kept coming back to me. Finally, I turned and asked, *"Do I know you, brother?"*

He smiled and said, *"Sir, you don't recognize me? I was your student."*

He took my name with respect and reminded me that he was from one of my very first batches. As soon as he said his name, I recalled—yes, he was that outspoken, confident, bindaas type of student. Not a topper, but someone with spark. If he had focused more, he could have scored very well. He smiled and said, *"Sir, you've stayed so fit! Still maintaining yourself so well."* I laughed and replied, *"Yes, I try. Gym, food, self-care—you know how it is. But you tell me, what are you doing now?"*

What he said next surprised me.

"Sir, after CLASS 10, when I joined 11th, I fell in love. The girl was from a Rajasthani family. Her family started pressuring her for

marriage very early. So I had to make a decision. I stopped studying after 12th and we got married through a court marriage." I was silent. He continued, *"Now we have two small children. I'm working at a local business, helping with accounts. Life is okay, but busy with responsibilities."* I nodded, listening carefully. But inside, my heart felt heavy. Here was a young boy who once had potential. A mind that could have gone far in commerce. But instead, he took life decisions very early—maybe out of love, maybe out of pressure, maybe just because no one guided him when it mattered most.

This wasn't just his story. It was a reflection of a larger problem.

If I introduced him to someone as my former student, they would be shocked. He looks like a different person today, tired, burdened, a family man who once could have been a leader or entrepreneur. The real question is:

Why did he make such life-altering decisions so early?

Was it purely his fault, or did our system miss a chance to guide him?

The truth is, our education system gives students too much unstructured free time, especially during 11th and 12th. While the syllabus covers subjects, no one covers life. There's no strong counseling, no real career mentoring, and absolutely no one to explain the emotional distractions that can delay or damage a student's future. And let's be honest, he's not the only one. Behind every early love story that turns into marriage at 18 or 19, there's often a missing teacher, mentor, or system that should have stepped in and said: *"Wait. Think. Focus. Your future is important."* Commerce education must become more than subjects and syllabus. It should become a support system that builds the student's career, mental health, emotional intelligence, and life vision. If we fail to engage our students in those crucial years, free time becomes a trap. And once a student takes a turn too early, sometimes he or she doesn't return to the road they were meant to walk on. This story is not about blame. It's a reminder that every student needs guidance before freedom becomes misdirection.

Let us not teach just accounts and economics. Let us teach how to live wisely, choose rightly, and grow strongly.

"Direction is so much more important than speed. Many are going nowhere fast."

Ethics Without Practice Is Just a Theory

But even when time is structured and lessons are delivered, there is something deeper that often goes missing in commerce education—ethics. As I look back on my years of teaching, I realize that while we teach business models, profits, and financial ratios, we rarely succeed in nurturing one simple yet powerful quality: conscience. I say this with a heavy heart because I have seen it unfold in real life. One of my former students, a bright and ambitious boy, came from a humble background. He lived in a crowded slum area but had big dreams of starting his own business. And he did. He set up a small production unit—right next to his own home. When I heard about it, I was filled with pride. A commerce student starting something of his own—that's the dream, isn't it?

A few days later, I happened to pass through his area and decided to visit. As I walked closer, a thick smell hung in the air. It was difficult to breathe. I felt a discomfort I couldn't ignore. When I asked him what was going on, he casually replied, *"Sir, just a small acrylic production setup.* It's doing well—good profit." His eyes were shining with excitement. But my heart sank. He had never asked the real questions: Is this the right place? Is this production harming the people living here? Is the profit coming at the cost of others' health?

This moment taught me something. Commerce education had taught him how to start a business, but not where to start one. It taught him to count profit, but not to question its price. He had the degree, the skill, and the motivation, but lacked the ethical compass. As I stood there, watching children play near the smoke-filled unit, a disturbing thought crossed my mind: Are we producing smart graduates but careless humans?

Commerce, after all, is not just about selling a ₹10 item for ₹30 and celebrating a ₹20 profit. It should also teach: Is it fair? Is it safe? Is it sustainable? These questions are not extra—they are essential. This isn't just one story. I have countless such examples. Another student of mine, now working in a private firm, once told me proudly, *"Sir, my duty is six hours. Once it's done, I don't care what happens after that."* His words echoed in my mind long after he left. This wasn't laziness. This was a mindset—a mindset that says, *"My job ends when the clock stops."*

Where did this mindset come from?

Perhaps from classrooms that only taught definitions and assignments, but never explained the human side of being an employee. We forget that whether you run a company or work in one, your values define your legacy. Ratan Tata once said, *"Businesses need to go beyond the interests of their companies to the communities they serve."* That spirit is missing in today's commerce classrooms. Ethics is often treated as a chapter in a textbook, not as a lens through which every decision must be seen. When we teach profit but forget people, when we praise success but ignore service, when we discuss markets but silence morality—we fail as educators.

Let us not forget the story of Ratan Tata, who once chose to continue the Tata Nano project despite criticism and financial strain, simply because he had given his word to the people of Gujarat. He stood by a promise, not for business gain, but for ethical integrity. And in doing so, he won something no money can buy trust.

Another story that stays with me is of Narayana Murthy, the founder of Infosys. In the early days of Infosys, when offered a deal that involved paying a bribe to secure a contract, he refused. Even when the company was struggling, he chose ethics over easy money. That one decision shaped the future of Infosys as one of India's most respected companies. His wife Sudha Murthy later said, *"Ethics may slow down your journey, but it makes your path cleaner and your sleep deeper."*

Why don't we tell these stories to our students?

Why do we teach them to balance accounts but not to balance ambition with empathy?

Why do we prepare them to answer clients but not to answer their conscience?

If we wish to build not just commerce graduates but good human beings, our lessons must change. Our case studies must talk about human impact, not just balance sheets. Our role plays must include ethical dilemmas, not just business strategies. And our exams must test courage, not just memory. Because, in the end, ethics is not a subject—it is a culture. And if we don't build it into education, life will build it the hard way.

And for commerce education, that time is now.

A System Full of Questions

As we stand at the intersection of what commerce education promises and what it actually delivers, one truth becomes clear: there is a wide gap between expectation and reality. As parents, we believe that if our child studies commerce for five years, they will understand the real world of commerce. As teachers, we think that even if we are sharing only bookish knowledge, it will still help students build their future. As students, many of us are enrolled in commerce because someone else made that choice—parents, peers, or society—hoping this path will lead somewhere. As policymakers, we assume that the reforms and rules we make are in the best interest of the student. But here is the truth: assumptions are not enough.

As a teacher and a writer, I want to ask the students:

Are you really learning something you'll apply in life?

Are you studying because it excites you, or because it was chosen for you?

Do you truly want to build your career in this stream?

To the parents:

Are you sending your child to college for five important years just to keep him or her "BUSY"?

Do you know how that time is being used? Have you checked what he or she are really gaining?

To the policymakers:

Don't you think your policies need a human touch—a real connection with the ground-level reality?

And to my fellow teachers, I ask with honesty:

Are you teaching just what's in the syllabus, or are you also teaching life?

Have you yourself experienced the banking systems, filed taxes, taken financial risks, worked in the business world, or is your teaching just words from a book?

Are we sharing knowledge that builds lives or only marks?

These are the questions that form the heart of this book

"Degree in Hand, Vision on Hold: Rethinking Commerce Education"

Yes, I talk about commerce more than other streams. That's because I belong to it. I have spent the most important years of my life living, learning, and teaching commerce. I connect deeply with commerce students their struggles, their confusions, and their silent dreams. That's why I chose to make commerce the central theme of this book. This book is not a revolution. It may not shake the system overnight. But if it can raise questions in a few hearts if it can bring awareness to even a few students, teachers, parents, and policymakers then it has fulfilled its purpose.

I do not write to criticize. I write to reflect.

I do not write to attack. I write to awaken.

Let this book be a mirror, not a hammer.

Let it be a torchlight, not a flame.

Let it be the beginning of a deeper thought that we must rethink how we prepare our children for life. Dear reader, as you continue through the next chapters, keep one question in mind:

"Am I part of the problem or part of the solution?"

If you are reading this book, you already care.

After reading these stories, one thing becomes clear: students are not always wrong; sometimes the system just doesn't know how to guide them. The boy who wanted to become a film director, the cricketer who gave up his dream, but landed in accountancy; they didn't choose commerce, commerce simply became their backup plan. These are not just stories. They are silent struggles, hidden behind B.Com timetables and lecture halls. Every story here reflects one common problem: no one asked them what they truly wanted. And even when students enter with talent or passion, there is often no one to nurture it. They adjust. They settle. They accept. Not because they're lazy but because they're lost. So, what should we ask now?

If so many students are confused, unmotivated, or simply disinterested... Where do we go from here? The answer lies in one direction: TEACHERS.

Because the right teacher can spot the lost spark, ask the right question, and give that one push that changes everything. In the next chapter, we'll stop blaming the students and start looking at the people who shape them. We'll ask a strong question: Are we building teachers who carry vision or just teachers who carry notes? Because when teachers teach with vision, even confused students can find their path.

So let's turn pages to explore more...

CHAPTER 4

THE MISSING MENTORS

In the previous chapters, we explored the real purpose of commerce education, the lack of clarity among students entering this stream, and how real-life outcomes often show a gap between what is taught and what is needed. But why is this happening? Why are we not building entrepreneurs, leaders, or innovators through commerce education?

One truth becomes clear: education is not just about syllabus or exams — it is about the people who deliver it. It is about the teachers.

If commerce students are graduating with degrees but without vision, without confidence, and without the mindset to build their own future, then we must ask: what kind of teachers are we preparing?

This chapter asks a simple but urgent question:

Are we building teachers with vision - or are we simply producing lecturers on an assembly line?

~ *The foundation of every state is the education of its youth.*~ - ***Diogenes***

One day, while thinking deeply about this, a strange image came to my mind - a factory.

Are we truly nurturing teachers with vision?

Or are we simply producing lecturers on an assembly line?

In my years of experience, I have observed certain clear patterns. Most commerce teachers today fall into three broad categories: permanent teachers with secured government-paid jobs, contract teachers working on clock-hour basis, and visiting faculty who come to deliver a few lectures and leave. But even before we discuss these categories, an even deeper question arises: How do these teachers actually become teachers?

The Traditional Path A Family of Teachers

In many families, teaching is not just a job. It's a tradition passed down like an old family recipe. The father is a teacher, the mother is a teacher, and even the uncle who once ran a small stationery shop ends up in teaching. It becomes a natural path, something everyone expects you to follow without even questioning it. From a young age, children in such families are told the same story: First do B.Com, then M.Com, after that go for B.Ed, clear NET or SET, and finally, get a Ph.D. That's the full package. Even if someone fails once or twice, it's okay. They're told to keep trying because that's the only way to get a teaching job. For them, it's not about passion. It's about finishing the steps one by one like completing levels in a game. Many even get jobs through community-based colleges—Hindu colleges, Muslim colleges, Christian colleges, or others—where knowing the right people sometimes works faster than sending a resume. Let's be honest here. These teachers are qualified. They have cleared the necessary exams. They have also gone through interviews. On paper, everything looks perfect.

But here's the question we often avoid asking: do they really understand the business world? Have they worked in the industry? Do they know what it means to run a business, take a risk, handle failure, or innovate in real time? And more importantly, can they teach students how to become entrepreneurs or leaders? With all due respect to every hardworking teacher, the reality is, many of them cannot. Not because they don't want to, but because they've never been there themselves. A quote I truly believe in says, *"A teacher affects eternity; he can never tell where his influence stops."* And that's exactly why this matters. Because if a teacher has never seen the real world, never experienced business beyond textbooks, then what are they really passing on?

Most of the time, they are teaching the same old theories, outdated concepts, and examples from the 90s. They enter the classroom with confidence, but their stories end with definitions, not decisions. They explain what a sole proprietorship is, but not how to actually run one. Students sit in these classes and wonder, *"How is this going to help me start a business or face the real world?"* The sad part is that our students today need more than just knowledge. They need courage. They need direction. They need real-life understanding. But many teachers have never experienced the pressure of filing GST, closing a business deal, handling a client, or even facing the fear of failure. One of my favourite quotes says,

"The mediocre teacher tells. The good teacher explains. The superior teacher demonstrates. The great teacher inspires." And this is where our system fails. We have so many teachers who tell and explain, but very few who inspire.

That's why we keep producing employees, not entrepreneurs. Followers, not leaders. Safe thinkers, not risk-takers. Until we change the way we hire and train teachers, this cycle will continue. If we only look at degrees, exams, and certificates while hiring, then we'll miss something even more important—experience and passion. A passionate teacher is not the one who just ticks all the boxes. A passionate teacher is someone who can stand in front of a class and say, *"I've been through this. Let me show you how it's done."*

I'm not writing this to blame anyone. I'm writing this to remind all of us that the future of our students depends on the kind of people who stand in front of them every day. Are we hiring teachers to just complete the syllabus? Or are we bringing in people who can light a spark in the minds of students?

The Passionate Teacher - Caught in a Broken System

Let's talk about the second kind of teacher.

These are the teachers who never really planned to be here. Some chose teaching because it was a secure option. Some entered the profession after not finding stability elsewhere. And some, despite entering accidentally, discovered that teaching was more than a job. It was a calling. I'm one of them. I had no teachers in my family. No childhood dream of standing at a blackboard. But once I began, I realized that nothing gave me more meaning than standing in front of a class and igniting minds. That's why I stayed. The path of such teachers is rarely smooth. They graduate, pursue their M.Com., and begin teaching in degree colleges, usually on a contract basis or clock-hour basis. They work across colleges, juggling lectures, while also preparing for NET, SET, B.Ed., or Ph.D. Their days are full of responsibilities; their nights are filled with assignments and hopes.

Many of them silently dream: *"If I keep performing, working hard, and staying visible, I'll eventually get a permanent post."* But reality has different plans. Year after year, they give NET. Again and again, they try SET. They collect certificates, complete research, apply for Ph.D., yet nothing permanent comes. One of my colleagues once said,

"If UGC had a loyalty card system, I would have received a free NET attempt by now."

Another joked,

"I've been in a relationship since I started applying for Ph.D. admissions. The relationship didn't work out, and neither did the Ph.D."

This is how passionate teachers cope with humor hiding heartbreak. They continue to do everything a full-time faculty member does: plan lectures, attend meetings, maintain exam records, coordinate committees, train juniors, motivate students, and build college culture. But every month, their bank balance reminds them they are still "TEMPORARY." They don't get stability. They don't get fair pay. They don't get appreciation. They only get told: *"Just wait. Be patient. Keep working."* But here's the bitter truth: passion cannot survive forever in a vacuum. When a teacher gives everything to an institution, but never receives recognition or growth, something slowly starts to break.

One day, that same teacher, who once used to arrive early, decorate the notice board, and take extra lectures with a smile, starts saying *"I don't have the energy anymore. I've already taught it all."*

This isn't laziness. This is emotional burnout, a quiet surrender that comes when passion is repeatedly ignored. And here's the tragedy: The system doesn't break the mediocre ones. It breaks the passionate ones.

They are the ones who gave more than they were asked.

They are the ones who went beyond the timetable.

They are the ones who stayed not for money, but for meaning.

Honestly, we give degrees for everything—M.Com, B.Ed., Ph.D., NET, SET. But where's the degree for passion? There should be a formal recognition—a symbolic certificate for those who gave their hearts to teaching, even when the system gave them nothing in return. Let's not forget: it is these teachers who train the future. But who is training and supporting them?

A System That Needs to Wake Up

If we don't uplift our passionate teachers financially, professionally, and emotionally, then slowly, but surely, their passion will die. Not in one moment, but over years of disappointment. And when that happens, we lose more than just one teacher—we lose the fire that once inspired hundreds. Education systems talk about "BUILDING THE NATION." But nations are not built by infrastructure alone. They are built by minds. And minds are built by teachers. So here's a humble truth: If we don't support the passionate teacher today, tomorrow's classrooms will be filled with teachers who only teach for the paycheck. And when that happens, education becomes a transaction, not a transformation. Let's not wait for that day. Let's bring back the respect, the recognition, and the reward that passionate teachers truly deserve.

When Teaching Becomes a Business: Showroom Lectures, Warehouse Hustles

Now let's talk about the third kind of teacher—the freelancers, the visiting faculty, the multi-tasking academic warriors. These are the teachers who hop from one college to another like Uber drivers switching rides. Morning in one college, afternoon in another, and evening in coaching classes or private tuitions. They don't carry a briefcase—they carry a timetable so tight, even Google Calendar begs for mercy. For them, college is not the main office—it's just the showroom. The real "WAREHOUSE"—where the income flows—is elsewhere: coaching centers, private institutes, home tuitions, or online batches. Let's be honest—some of them are really good. They deliver crisp, stylish lectures, crack a few jokes, wrap the concept like a gift, and leave before the chalk dust settles. Students love them. Principals admire their energy. But scratch the surface, and another layer appears—the image-builders. They are not in education for money or for meaning. They're here for reputation. For the title. For the photo with a mic. And here's where the reality check begins.

The Clock-Hour Hustler - A Real-Life Eye-Opener

One of my friends, let's call him Mr. X, was working as a visiting faculty across three colleges and taking private coaching classes in the evening. Out of curiosity, I once asked, *"Bhai, how much do you earn from college?"* He laughed. *"College? That's not for earning. That's just to maintain status. My income starts after 11 a.m.!"* I once looked at his schedule. From 7 a.m. to 10 p.m., back-to-back lectures. I was shocked. He had a Ph.D., talent, and passion—but that passion was more for self-growth than for student growth. He gave a lecture in college like a movie trailer—fast-paced, flashy, and over in minutes. But the full movie? That was reserved for his private classes where students paid a premium.

The Dual Role Drama - Where Ethics Take a Nap

Some setups are so perfectly unethical, they'd impress a scammer. These teachers teach in the college from 9 to 10 a.m. and by 10:15, they've lured the same students into their own tuition classes down the road. A student once told me, *"Sir, our teacher just reads slides in college. But in private class—wow! He's a rockstar!"* And I thought, so basically, college students get the free trial, and coaching kids get the premium version. Sometimes I wonder—if the college just paid ₹200 more per lecture, would we finally get the full version in class?

The Comedy of Clock-Hour Contracts

There's this unspoken joke among visiting faculty: *"We're not teachers. We're delivery partners—Swiggy of education."* You ask them, *"Are you free tomorrow?" and they'll reply, "Which slot? Morning batch, noon batch, or twilight zone?"* Another friend said, *"Bhai, I'm not looking for a job. I'm building a brand."* That's when I realized—for many, teaching has become a personal startup. Which would've been great—if the students were investors, not unpaid subscribers.

Dear Teacher: Not Every Student Can Afford Your Coaching Class

Let's be clear about this. Not every student can afford ₹15,000 for a private batch. Not every parent can pay double for the same teacher they already paid college fees for. You may be a brilliant educator, but if you're giving your best version only to those who pay extra, then you're not a teacher. You're a businessman wearing a professor's coat. College is not your advertisement board. It is a classroom. And classrooms come with responsibility. A Gentle Reality Check for the "IMAGE PROFESSORS" Remember your first lecture? That nervous energy, that passion to connect, that dream to become someone students admire? Now look in the mirror. Are you that person today? Because right now, some of you are walking into class like you're hosting a one-minute Instagram reel. No preparation, no real teaching, just vibes and volume. If this hurts, good. That means your spark is still alive. That means you still care. Let's be very clear: The education system has its flaws. Salaries are low. Recognition is rare. But if that becomes an excuse to turn your college into a marketing platform, then students will stop respecting the profession.

A Message to Teachers - With Love and a Little Fire

You might be doing 5 jobs to survive, and we understand that. But don't let survival kill sincerity.

Give your best even when no one is watching. Because someone is watching: That shy girl who dreams of becoming a CA, that lost boy who needs one spark to find his path. You might be the only teacher in their life who can make a difference. And if you're reading this and remembering a time you used to give your best in class, then this chapter isn't criticizing you. It's calling you back.

In the End…

The real test of a teacher is not how many students they attract to their coaching class.

The real test is this:

"When your students become teachers, do they try to teach like you?"

A Little Story - A Window into the Mindset

As I was writing this chapter, one memory came strongly to mind. Years ago, I was working in an institution. The person in charge there was a lady - a housewife - whose residence was just near the college. One day, the management asked her a simple question:

"Madam, today you came in late. Do you know which teachers were present? Which students came on time? Who was late?"

And her reply was unforgettable:

"Sir, my kitchen window faces the college gate. From my kitchen, while making tea, I saw who was coming in and who was not!"

I could not stop laughing that day. But behind that humor, a deep truth struck me. When one person tries to play multiple roles - without full dedication to either - somewhere, something will surely be compromised. And this is exactly what happens when we bring in "IMAGE TEACHERS" or *"part-time badge seekers"* into serious education roles.

"When you try to ride two horses, you often fall between them."

For some, the goal is to wear the "BADGE" of a professor - not to mentor students.

And this links directly to the message of this book.

If teachers themselves are entering with a "TIME IS MONEY" mindset, or with an "IMAGE POLISHING" mindset, or with no real industry experience - how can we expect commerce students to come out with a vision to become leaders, creators, entrepreneurs?

They will naturally come out with: Degree in Hand, but Vision on Hold.

When Teachers Become Data Entry Operators

There's a strange trend in our education system: the more we talk about improving teaching quality, the more non-teaching work we dump on teachers. Somewhere in the government files, a teacher's job description must read *"Primary duty: paperwork. Secondary duty: if time permits, teach students."*

A teacher's modern-day to-do list.

First comes the "SARAAL PROCESS" which, by the way, sounds like it should be something simple (after all, 'saral' means easy). But the reality? It's like calling a 1000-piece jigsaw puzzle "QUICK FUN." SARAAL actually stands for Systematic Administrative Reforms for Achieving Learning, but ironically, it takes away so much teaching time that achieving actual learning becomes a challenge. This registration process for every 11th-standard student can eat up almost a month of a class teacher's life.

Then comes UDISE and UDISE Validation Unified District Information System for Education Plus. The "PLUS" here means "PLUS HEADACHE." First, we enter every student's personal details. Then we verify them. Sounds straightforward, until you find that some student's name has been entered as "RAHUL" in one record and "RAGHUL" in another, or their birthdate makes them 53 years old on paper. Fixing these errors takes time, patience, and occasionally a detective's skill set.

This year, we have a new guest: APAAR: Automated Permanent Academic Account Registry. Sounds high-tech, right? In reality, it's more like creating a "NETFLIX ACCOUNT" for every student, except you need their Aadhaar, phone number, address, parents' details, and possibly the name of their neighbor's dog. All this, of course, happens during college hours because the required documents are in college, and so, once again, teaching gets pushed to the background.

And let's not forget, amidst all this, we also manage parent meetings, exam supervision, open days, and the occasional *"Sir, why do you need this information?"* interrogation session from parents.

Now imagine a teacher plans to explain a topic like the French Revolution in an interesting way. But just as they start, a reminder pops up: *"Today is the last day for UDISE validation."* The lesson on *"Storming of the Bastille"* is replaced with "Storming of the Staffroom" as teachers rush to meet deadlines. It's no surprise that many students feel their actual learning happens in coaching classes, not because college teachers don't want to teach well, but because they are drowning in forms, portals, and verifications. The solution is simple: automate all these processes. Attendance, data entry, verification: all of it. Let teachers do what they were hired to do: teach. If a college teacher spends most of their time filling forms instead of filling minds, the **"DEGREE IN HAND"** will always come with **"VISION ON HOLD."**

Because, honestly, the only registry teachers should be worried about is the one where they register knowledge in a student's mind — not the APAAR, UDISE, or SARAAL servers.

What Makes a Good Teacher?

Over the years, I have seen that teachers play one of the most critical roles in shaping students - sometimes even more than the curriculum or the system itself. I would like to share some real-life experiences about teachers - the good and the not-so-good - which taught me valuable lessons. One of my friends teaches theory subjects. His language is very "MUMBAI-STYLE" - casual, informal. Initially, I used to think, *"Is this professional? Will this person be able to deliver a proper lecture?"*

But to my surprise, students connected with him beautifully. They understood him. There was a sense of comfort and relatability in his style. And in my view - that is what makes a good teacher: a teacher who can engage students and make them feel involved.

On the other hand, we had another teacher who was extremely knowledgeable - but spoke very slowly. She was highly talented, but had issues with delivery. The sad truth is - no matter how much expertise you have, if you cannot engage students, they will not be able to connect. The market will not accept such teaching. Students naturally prefer teachers whose style resonates with them - who can keep them involved and active. Then we had some teachers who used storytelling techniques - they would explain concepts through stories, use keywords, and simplify tough topics. Naturally, these teachers were very successful in engaging students.

It doesn't matter whether we are permanent teachers, contract-based teachers, or clock-hour teachers, what matters is that we must connect with students. We must understand them, help them understand, and remember that teaching is a responsibility – we are building the foundation for their future. Unfortunately, I have also had some bad experiences with teachers. Once, at an assessment center, I saw a teacher checking theory papers at an incredibly fast speed. I asked, *"How are you checking so fast? Are you reading the answers?"*

The reply was shocking:

"Oh, everyone writes the same thing – what's the point of reading every answer in detail?"

Now think – students work hard the entire year, and when they finally write their exams, some teachers mark their papers without even reading them carefully. This must change. We need more care and responsibility in how we assess students. I have also seen teachers who only teach selected answers. I once asked such a teacher, *"Why aren't you covering the full syllabus?"*

The reply was: **"Why should I? Students only want exam-related questions and answers. That's what I give them - I make them memorize it."** But is this really what a teacher should be doing? Is this fulfilling their true responsibility? Absolutely not. A teacher's role is to help students understand the full subject - not just train them to pass exams. I have also seen teachers in exam centers who would either be too lenient and allow cheating, or too strict.

Now here's the question - should we allow copying? If we do, what happens to those students who have genuinely worked hard and prepared honestly? If we believe that every student should pass, the solution is not to let them cheat - the solution is to teach them well enough so that they are capable of passing on their own. Teachers have a huge responsibility. Their role is not just to complete the syllabus - it is to shape lives, values, confidence, and the very future of students.

To the Teachers Just Recollect

The Silent Spark When Routine Replaces Passion

The First Day Fire Remember That Feeling?

Every teacher remembers his or her first day in college: the excitement, the nervousness, the feeling of stepping into a classroom not just to teach, but to transform. You had ideas. You wanted to make the subject interesting. You wanted your students to see commerce not just as theory, but as a way of thinking. You prepared late at night, practiced lectures, searched for current examples, and even tried to crack a joke or two. You were not just a teacher. You were a dreamer with a marker in hand.

The Unexpected Shift When Passion Becomes Process

But somewhere down the line, something changed. It wasn't sudden. It was slow… like chalk dust settling on an empty bench. Maybe it was the pressure of completing the portion. Maybe it was the growing file of non-teaching duties. Maybe it was just life. Without realizing it, the same notes came out again. The the same subject, the same file, the same lectures. And that *"let me try something new today"* voice got quieter. Students still respect you. They still listen. But deep down you know it too, you're not enjoying it the way you used to.

The Sugarcane Machine Analogy: A Gentle Reminder

You know the sugarcane juice machine on the street? You put the cane in… crank the lever… juice comes out. Every time. Same motion. Same result. A few teachers start feeling the same: Put the topic in, say the lines, take attendance, and finish.

And yes, we know this.

it's not your fault.

It's the system.

It's the pressure.

It's the repetition.

But it's also a silent call:

"Hey, where did your spark go?"

The Story of Ma'am Who Once Lit Up the Room

There's a ma'am I remember when she joined. Students waited for her lecture. She used to relate topics to real life, discuss markets, make finance fun. But over the years… her voice slowed down.

Her examples became old. Her energy faded. One day I asked her, *"Ma'am, why don't you try some new case studies?"* She smiled and said, *"Dear, where do I get the time now? And anyway… I've already taught everything."* That hit me, because that's the exact moment I realized she hadn't lost her talent. She had just accepted the routine.

The Spark Is Still There; it just needs oxygen

Let's be clear. We're not blaming anyone. In fact, this is an ode to every teacher who once had fire in their eyes. We know what this profession demands. It's not easy. Sometimes you teach with a headache. Sometimes you motivate others while you feel demotivated. But still, you show up. And that's where hope lies, because the spark never dies.

It just waits.

It is for a workshop.

For a new topic.

For a curious student who asks something unexpected.

And suddenly... you smile again.

You remember why you chose this.

You Still Matter. A Lot.

NET-SET and Ph.D. – A Never-Ending Race for Teachers

"Exams test memory, not mastery. Experience tests mastery, not memory."

Every teacher knows this pain: after teaching for 8–10 years in colleges, suddenly they decide, *"Now I will clear NET or SET."* But the challenge is this: when you're fresh out of M.Com., you're in touch with all subjects. But when you've been teaching Accounts or Economics for a decade, your mind has become a specialist factory. You're a master of one. Then NET-SET comes like a school inspector saying, *"Beta, now tell me everything: Economics, Marketing, Management, even a dash of Mathematics."* The teacher stares at the question paper and thinks, *"Boss, I haven't touched this since George Bush was President!"* This is the irony. Society believes that a teacher knows everything—like a human Google. If you teach Commerce, people expect you to be an expert in Economics, Law, Accounts, Tax, Management, Advertisement, and Marketing. But the truth is simple: colleges appoint teachers for one subject. An Accounts teacher is an Accounts expert, not an Encyclopedia. So, when an experienced teacher sits for NET-SET, yes, they score well in their own subject. But in other areas? The marks fall like Sensex on a bad Monday. Meanwhile, fresh graduates join coaching centers, study only for exams, and clear NET-SET in one go. The result? The veteran keeps trying again and again, while the newcomer gets the golden ticket.

One senior teacher once joked to me,

"By the time I clear NET, my own students will be examiners!"

Another added,

"I don't fear retirement. I fear failing this exam one more time."

So what happens next? These senior teachers, tired of repeated attempts, finally sacrifice and say, *"Forget it. Let me go for Ph.D."* But even that is no cakewalk. Ph.D. is long, costly, and draining. You pay lakhs in fees, spend years in research, and still there's no guarantee of timely completion. By the time the degree arrives, the teacher's passion has often faded. This creates a vicious cycle. Juniors get recognition faster, seniors lose motivation, and the system loses its gems. Imagine a teacher with 12 years of classroom experience losing out to someone with zero experience but a fresh NET certificate. It's like saying:

"A new driver with a learner's license is better than a man who has driven trucks for 20 years."

Ridiculous, right? But that's exactly how the system treats teachers. The University Grants Commission (UGC) needs to wake up here. Experienced teachers should not be judged on the same platform as beginners. Their years of teaching, mentoring, and guiding students must count as much as written exams do. Otherwise, more teachers will think twice before joining this profession.

And if our system continues to make experienced teachers run like students, we will lose the very minds that once trained others to think. So here's the real question we must ask: Do we want teachers who inspire classrooms, or teachers who only collect certificates?

So dear teacher, if while reading this, you remembered your own lectures, your first day, your old spark, then know this: the candle is still burning. You are not just a teacher. You are a spark that has lit up hundreds of lives. Even if you feel tired, even if the system tests your patience, remember, one student, somewhere, is still waiting for your best version to show up. Let us not teach just to finish the syllabus. Let us teach to finish doubts, to finish fear, to finish ignorance. The world doesn't need syllabus-completers; it needs passion-reigniters.

"A good teacher doesn't just prepare students for exams. They prepare them for life."

"A teacher is not one who gives answers,

but one who sparks curiosity.

Not one who completes the syllabus,

but one who awakens the mind."

And yet, dear teachers, we know the truth. Your spark often battles a storm. Low pay, endless exams, clock-hour contracts, politics in recruitment, and pressure to prove yourself again and again—it can drain even the strongest heart. But don't let the system steal your enthusiasm. Because education is not built by classrooms or policies—it is built by you. At the same time, we cannot ignore the bigger question: who designed this broken journey for teachers? Who made a system where passion struggles, and paperwork wins? Who decided that loyalty and experience count less than certificates?

That is where we must now turn our attention. Teachers fight daily battles, but the war is shaped by those who design the rules. If teachers are the mentors of the classroom, then the real makers of the system sit far above them: in universities, in commissions, in policy rooms.

But I would add: If we treat today's teachers as we treated yesterday's, we may lose tomorrow's classrooms. So before we point fingers at teachers, we must ask who built this machinery in which they are stuck. Who are the real *"makers of the system"*?

Let's turn the pageand meet them.

CHAPTER 5

TO THE MAKERS OF THE SYSTEM A WAKE - UP CALL FOR REAL REFORM

Time for a Revival

To understand where we are, we must also understand where it all began. The education system that we follow today—structured, uniform, exam-centric—wasn't designed to produce thinkers. It was never meant to create leaders, innovators, or entrepreneurs. It was designed by the British for one simple reason: to produce obedient clerks and government servants who would assist the empire. The student wasn't supposed to build something of his own. He was supposed to fill ledgers, follow orders, and ensure the administrative machinery worked smoothly. That was the colonial aim. And tragically, that legacy never truly left us. Before this imported system, India had a different soul. A child born in a goldsmith's family would learn the art of jewellery. A child from a carpenter's house would craft wood with precision and pride. Potters, weavers, farmers, artists: our education was skill-based, locally rooted, and spiritually fulfilling. Education was not about passing exams. It was about mastering a craft.

Not about chasing jobs. But about building value. Not about survival. But about creation. But post-colonial India, in the name of modernization, continued the British structure. The result? An entire generation that believes that the highest purpose of learning is to become a government employee. That thinks success is measured by job security, not by innovation or independence. And now, it's 2025. We still see families celebrate a government job more than a startup. We still measure intelligence by how well a student clears competitive exams—not how well he understands the world around him.

That colonial hangover needs to end, because we're no longer subjects of an empire. We're the citizens of a nation with the youngest population, unlimited digital potential, and centuries of entrepreneurial spirit in our DNA. It's time for a revival. A revival of our original mindset. A revival of courage over compliance. A revival of the carpenter's pride, the artisan's mastery, the farmer's wisdom. A revival of learning that leads to doing, not just applying.

Education must no longer be a preparation to serve.

It must be a preparation to lead, build, and create.

And for that, we don't just need policy change. We need purpose change. Let the next chapter of India's education story be written not with colonial ink, but with the dreams of a new, self-reliant generation. Because the real independence will begin not when we change our syllabus, ... but when we change our mindset.

The Policy Loop :

"A system is not broken when it fails once. It is broken when it continues failing, and we pretend everything is fine."

We now shift our attention to the makers of this system—the policy designers, the education framers—because the problem is no longer just about delivery. It is about design.

The students entering this system are young, full of dreams, energy, and curiosity. But what happens to that energy after fifteen to twenty years of formal education? Most of them walk out either confused about what to do or fearful that they're not "QUALIFIED ENOUGH" for life. Our education system has unknowingly become a long, winding tunnel—with no clarity of when the light will arrive. And here's the sad irony: while the world is moving at lightning speed, our students are being told to "PREPARE SLOWLY." Prepare for what? And until when?

Let's pause and look at the real stories that say it all.

Story 1

Sameer left education after SSC. While most of his friends were still trying to solve accounting problems and memorize business law definitions, he was in a dusty carpentry workshop learning to sand wood, take orders, and deal with customers. That was his business school. In five years, he opened his own furniture studio. Today, he employs three commerce graduates—yes, graduates— who handle his accounts, social media, and taxes. He once told me with a smirk, "SIR, I DIDN'T EVEN CLEAR HSC, BUT NOW I SIGN THE SALARIES OF THOSE WHO DID M.COM." And he wasn't joking. The system produced employees, but life produced the entrepreneur.

Story 2

Ravi's story is just as revealing. He dropped out in the ninth standard and started helping at his uncle's tea stall. His friend Shubham continued with graduation, then MBA, and is now preparing for competitive exams. By the time Shubham completed another mock test, Ravi had opened three chai cafés with Wi-Fi, QR-code payments, and influencer marketing. Shubham once tried to explain revenue models to Ravi, who smiled and said, *"You design PowerPoints. I design profits."* One holds a degree in business. The other runs one.

Story 3

Imran, who joined a salon at sixteen, had no college degree, but a sharp understanding of people. Today, he owns a grooming studio that caters to social media influencers and professionals. When someone once asked him where he studied business, he replied, *"On the street where every customer teaches what no syllabus can."* Meanwhile, a marketing graduate working for him struggles to make a reel that gets more than 100 views.

Story 4

Ayesha started applying mehendi at age 15. Her first few designs looked like confused maps. One aunty even asked,

"Is this a flower or a fingerprint?" But she didn't give up. She practiced on everyone—friends, cousins, neighbours—who didn't run away fast enough. By 19, she had brides waiting weeks just to book her. She now runs a beauty parlour called Ayesha Artistry. When someone once asked her, *"Did you do a diploma in beauty?"* she smiled and said, *"No diploma. Just deadlines and brides who can't risk bad mehendi."*

Story 5

Karan grew up in a family-run farsan shop. His childhood memories smelled like frying oil and tasted like sev. One day, he said, *"Let's name our farsan and sell it online."* His father laughed and said, *"Snacks don't need branding. They just need salt."* Karan didn't listen. He made a logo, designed pouches, opened an Instagram page, and renamed the shop SnackShack. Now he ships their spicy chiwda across three states. His dad still fries the snacks. Karan fries the algorithms.

Story 6

Sneha started painting diyas with her grandmother. What began as a festive chore became her creative spark. She began painting themes: Bollywood, cartoons, even football clubs. One year, she put up a small stall at a flea market. A customer bought 30 diyas and said, *"This is better than the ones in malls."* That day, her business was born. Today, *"Glow by Sneha" is* a seasonal brand with pre-orders every Diwali. When asked how she markets them, she says, *"I light hearts before I light homes."*

Story 7

Mansi loved making chocolates at home. Her family said, *"Keep it as a hobby."* But she couldn't stop. She experimented with flavours, shapes, and fillings. Her bestseller? Chili Guava Dark Chocolate, which sounds weird but sells out every Valentine's Day. Today, Mansi's Melt is a homegrown chocolate brand with custom gift boxes and corporate orders. A customer asked, *"Is this made in a real factory?"*

She replied, *"No. It's made with real love."*

Story 8

Amaan worked in a small perfume shop. He loved how scents triggered emotions. One customer said, *"This reminds me of my grandfather."* That inspired him. He created a perfume line called ScentStory, with names like First Rain, Childhood Garden, and Old Library. No advertising; just emotion. Every bottle comes with a handwritten tag: Smells like something you forgot. Today, people don't just buy his perfumes. They revisit memories.

And Now We Have Story 9

Then there's Pooja, the picture-perfect student. She did everything right. B.Com, M.Com, NET, SET, Ph.D. coursework, even completed her thesis. But at twenty-nine, she is still waiting for a permanent job. She once told me, *"Sir, I followed the map the system gave me. But it led me nowhere."* She had degrees, certificates, and medals, but no direction. This was because the system trained her to prepare, not to begin.

Across India, the system may vary slightly from state to state, but one thing remains common: the long duration. It takes nearly twenty years for a student to go from their first classroom to their first paycheck. And this isn't because learning needs that long. It's because the system does. While the world outside is fast-forwarding, we are still stuck in pause. Teenagers around the globe are becoming coders at thirteen, YouTubers at fourteen, and startup founders at seventeen. They are building brands, writing books, launching businesses. And here, our students are still writing essays on the "IMPORTANCE OF CLEANLINESS" and attending lectures on outdated concepts. We have created a system that values time spent over skills gained. It's not about what you understand; it's about how many years you've sat through. And by the time many students finish sitting, they've forgotten how to stand up for themselves. Our universities have slowly turned into degree factories. Assignments are submitted. Exams are passed. Gowns are worn. Photos are clicked. But what happens after that? Most students are clueless. They don't know if they want a job, a business, or yet another degree. They only know that they must keep studying, because stopping would mean facing a world they were never prepared for. This chapter is not an attack. But it is a mirror. If you are a policy maker, a curriculum designer, or a framework developer, this is your moment of reflection. You don't just shape syllabi. You shape lives. The policies you design today determine who our students become tomorrow.

One Size Doesn't Fit All

Not every student is interested in playing a five-day Test match. Some just want a quick, energetic T20. And that's perfectly fine. It's time to accept that long-term education is not the only path. There are students who love the depth of three-year or five-year degree programs, and there are others who want short, focused, skill-based courses that help them start earning quickly. Today's generation needs options, not obligations.

Responsibility Towards Students: Give Them a Choice, Not a Chain

We Should be honest, some students are not made for marathon learning. They are sprinters, not joggers. But what happens in most colleges? The sprinter is forced to run a marathon, and halfway through, he's either bored, burnt out, or bunking class. We've all seen that one student in class who says, *"I don't even know why I'm doing this course. I just landed here."* And the topper next to him looks at him like, *"If you're not serious, why are you even here?"*There's always this tension between long-term and short-term learners, as if one is right, and the other is wrong. But both are just different. That's it. Some students want full-time graduation, postgraduation, research, and more. Great! But others want a 6-month graphic design course, a 1-year hospitality program, or a certification in social media marketing, and they want to start their careers now. So why don't we build systems for both?

We give them the same curriculum. same exams, and expect the same outcomess. That's like telling a 2-wheeler rider to pass a truck-driving test. Let's also talk about outcome. Even after a 3-year degree, many students say,

"Now I have to do an internship to get experience."

"Now I have to do an extra course to improve my communication."

"Now I need a job-oriented certification."

Why? Why should they need more after completing a full degree? Imagine you buy a fully-loaded car, top model, all features. You expect it to be ready for the road, right? But what if the seller says, *"Now you need to buy the seats, the tires, and the steering separately"?* That's exactly what our current education system is doing. Our degree must produce complete, self-sufficient students, not just certificate-holders who need more updates to function.

Responsibility Towards Parents: Make Education Affordable, Not Unbearable

Dear policy makers,, parents are not just "GUARDIANS" on school forms. They are the silent sponsors of this entire system. They may not attend meetings in air-conditioned halls, but they attend every fee receipt, EMI slip, and stationery bill. While we talk about educational reforms, parents are busy calculating whether they can afford the next academic year. Let's be real: some parents are working double shifts, skipping family functions, and delaying their own dreams just to send their children to college. Yet, we build systems that say, *"Pay now. Intern later. Job? Maybe."* Education should not feel like booking a 5-star hotel and ending up with room service charges that are more than the stay.

Can we build a system where:

Parents don't need to take loans to fund "EXTRA CERTIFICATIONS"?

Installments and flexibility aren't only available in malls and coaching classes.

Let's not make parents feel punished for wanting the best for their child.

A joke often heard in middle-class homes:

"Beta, you study well so that your child can go to a cheaper school."

That's not funny anymore. That's painful.

Education must not just fit the child's brain. It must also fit the parent's wallet.

Responsibility To Teachers: Support Those Who Deliver the Change

We cannot talk about educational reforms and ignore those who are expected to implement them — our teachers. We have passionate, talented, committed teachers across India. But we also have a system that often treats them like fillers: temporary appointments, clock-hour contracts, unclear job security, and irregular payments. In earlier chapters, we have already said this: when a teacher loses hope, the classroom loses direction. A passionate teacher can light up futures. But only if they are not overworked, underpaid, and constantly "WAITING FOR CONFIRMATION."

Policy makers must ask:

Are we appointing teachers fairly, or only when there's a vacancy crisis?

Are we giving them growth, dignity, and long-term security?

Are we expecting them to carry the weight of the NEP without even training them properly?

A teacher once said,

"I'm teaching entrepreneurship to students, but I can't afford to start my own life."

That says everything.

If we want real reform, we must first make teaching a respected profession again, with better pay scales, fair appointments, mental support, and modern training. Let's not burn out our teachers in the name of "RESPONSIBILITY." Let's empower them to deliver.

Responsibility Towards Society: Build Doers, Not Just Degree Holders

A strong education policy doesn't just benefit students; it shapes society. But when degrees don't lead to confidence, when education doesn't lead to independence, and when learning doesn't lead to earning, we don't just lose one person's potential, we lose the progress of a generation. A society full of educated but confused individuals is not developed. It is frustrated. We see graduates who can write a dissertation but can't write a simple email. Students who have a 9-point GPA but freeze in job interviews. Youth who know everything about marketing theories but nothing about marketing themselves.

Is this the outcome we want?

Imagine a society where students graduate, start businesses, innovate, create jobs, help others grow — that's not just economic growth. That's cultural revival. The best education system is not the one that creates the most toppers. It's the one that creates the most contributors.

Let's stop mass-producing degrees.

Let's start nurturing direction.

The Policy

We all agree that our old education system needed change, and the New Education Policy brought that change. At least on paper, it did. The NEP is modern, flexible, and filled with good intentions. But here's the real question: has it been implemented the way it was imagined? Let's understand this with a simple example. Imagine you buy the latest smart TV with 4K resolution, voice control, and Bluetooth features. But you keep it in a room that still has an old antenna, dusty switches, and no Wi-Fi. Can you really enjoy what that smart TV offers? That's exactly what's happening with NEP. The policy is advanced, but the ground-level system — our colleges, our infrastructure, our teachers — is still operating with an outdated mindset. I have personally attended several workshops and seminars during the NEP launch in Maharashtra. Many teachers walked out of the sessions saying things like, *"I didn't understand much, but I'll Google it later,"* or *"Maybe someone will explain it on YouTube."* When the very people responsible for delivering this policy don't fully understand it, how can we expect it to succeed in the classroom? And here's something even more important to ask — if NEP is designed to make education more engaging and student-friendly, then why is student attendance in colleges going down instead of going up? Shouldn't a modern policy bring students closer to learning, not push them away? These are questions we must ask, not with blame, but with the hope to do better. Because even the best policy needs the right people, the right tools, and the right mindset to truly bring change.

When Education Becomes a Business

"Education is not the filling of a pail, but the lighting of a fire."

– W.B. Yeats

One bitter truth we must accept is this: education is slowly turning into a marketplace. The moment the New Education Policy (NEP) was announced, something unusual happened—a flood of textbooks hit the market. Major subjects, minor subjects, electives—every corner of the syllabus suddenly had a book. Earlier, a B.Com. student would manage with six books. Now, the same student is expected to buy eleven or twelve. Who pays for this? The parents. Instead of asking how the NEP will improve quality, we first saw how it created business opportunities. Book writers, publishers, coaching classes, all found new ways to package the same old content. The thick textbook of yesterday has been cut into thin slices today. The surprising part? Each slice now costs ₹100, ₹200, sometimes ₹300. And when you open these books, much of the content feels recycled. Old wine in new bottles. Or let's say, old syllabus in new covers. It makes one wonder: Are we creating a better system, or just a bigger market?

Let us be clear: we are not here to criticize the NEP outright. We are not even in a position to judge its final outcome, because true results take years. All we can do today is observe the early patterns. And what we see is troubling: a policy meant to improve learning has already become a business in disguise.

This is not a blame game. This is only a humble reminder to policymakers:

Please measure outcomes regularly. Track what the NEP is actually doing to classrooms, to students, and to parents. Ensure that the long-term impact is positive. Because if we don't measure, we may one day realize we created paperwork and profits, but not progress.

And education is too important to be left unmeasured. Now that we have spoken about teachers and policymakers, there is one more group without which education cannot exist: the students themselves. Policies can guide, teachers can inspire, parents can sacrifice, but at the end of the day, it is the student who must transform knowledge into action. The next chapter is about them: their responsibility toward learning, their duty toward themselves, and their silent rebellion against a system that often underestimates them. Some students rise and transform beautifully. Others carry a fire of frustration, a quiet resistance, waiting to be heard.

Victor Hugo said,

"He who opens a school door, closes a prison."

But remember that when students open that door, they must also walk through it with courage.

So let's turn more pages to explore more…

CHAPTER 6

THE SYSTEM NEEDS SCHOOLING

Student Responsibility - Transforming Graduation Into a Journey of Growth

In the earlier chapters, we explored how commerce education today often lacks direction. Many students drift into degrees without clear goals, without knowing why they are studying what they are studying. We saw how the current system sometimes produces degree holders without purpose, and that needs to change. Now, in this chapter, we take that thought one step forward: What should students themselves do to change this? Because no education system, no teacher, no parent - can transform a student unless the student takes responsibility for their own learning and growth.

Graduation should not be about simply collecting a piece of paper. It should be about becoming a better version of yourself - skilled, confident, and prepared for the real world. One of the most important, yet often ignored, elements in this process is language - especially English in today's global industry. It is not just a subject; it is a skill that can open doors and shape your personality.

Let me share a real-life example from my experience as a teacher.

Language as a Key to Transformation

I once had a student from a Gujarati-medium background. He was pursuing graduation but struggled with English. His classmates would often tease him when he spoke in broken English. One day, I told him, *"Beta, if you are not comfortable in English, it's okay; speak in the language you are confident in."* But his response surprised me, and became an example I now share with many of my students.

He replied, *"Sir, I know I come from a Gujarati-medium background. We speak Gujarati at home. But I don't want to settle for a low-profile job just because of my poor English. I want to improve my language during my graduation so that I can compete in the industry."* This determination touched me deeply. He did not take graduation as a formality; he took it as an opportunity to transform himself. A few years later, I received a call from him. This time, with a polished and confident voice, he said, *"Sir, this is your Gujarati student from Vasai. I am now working as a Manager in a big firm in Canada!"*

That is the power of mindset and consistent effort. Graduation is the phase where a student can reinvent himself or herself. Yes, the process is difficult. It requires consistent work — not just in academics, but in improving skills like communication, personality, and confidence. To all students: Don't treat your degree as just a certificate. Use these years to become a better version of yourself. Language, especially, should not be limited to theory. It is the key to building an impressive personality and standing tall in the professional world. And I would add — the first world you can change with education is your own self.

The Power of Extra-Curricular Participation

In my journey as an educator, one thing has always stood out to me:

The most successful students I've seen are not always the toppers — they are the ones who actively participate in extra-curricular activities. Why? Because the stage, the mic, the events — they do what books alone cannot. They help students develop public speaking, leadership, and most importantly, confidence. Academic success is important, but overall development is a must. A degree without personality and communication is like a car without fuel — it may look good, but it won't take you far.

Let me share another real-life story from my experience.

A few years ago, a very shy student joined our college. He was so reserved, he hardly spoke to his friends. Public speaking or leadership was the last thing anyone expected from him. One day, we were preparing for a fashion show. We needed someone to walk on stage dressed as Mahatma Gandhi - just a simple walk, portraying peace. But no one was available for the role. I noticed this shy student sitting nearby, quietly watching the practice. I approached him and said, *"Beta, will you help us? Just walk on stage once. We'll find someone else tomorrow."*

He was nervous and kept saying, *"No sir, no sir, I can't do it."* But I encouraged him gently, and finally, he agreed - just for that day and my motivation made him perform on the final day too. When the final event came, magic happened. The moment this boy walked on stage, dressed as Mahatma Gandhi with a stick, the entire crowd erupted in applause. The cheers boosted his confidence in an instant. That was a turning point. After that event, the same student started participating in almost every college event - fashion shows, skits, anchoring, organizing. From a shy boy to an active, confident student - his transformation was inspiring.

This is the power of activities. One opportunity, one step outside your comfort zone, can change everything. To all students: **Don't just chase marks - chase moments that can change you.** Participate in activities, take the mic, walk the stage, work behind the scenes - each experience shapes your personality.

As **Eleanor Roosevelt** said:

"Do one thing every day that scares you."

And trust me — the stage is a great place to start.

Understanding the New Education Policy (NEP) — A Student's Responsibility

It is very important for today's students to understand that education is not just about attending classes or passing exams. True education is about understanding what you are learning, why you are learning it, and how you can apply it in real life. One of the best examples of this is the New Education Policy (NEP). The NEP was introduced with the vision of giving students greater flexibility — allowing them to choose subjects they are truly interested in. If a subject is not available in their college, they can take that subject from another college.

But in reality, very few students are making use of this flexibility. The question is — how many students have actually joined two or more colleges to take different subjects? Very few. Why? Because there is a big gap between what was envisioned under NEP and what is actually happening on the ground. One of the main reasons for this gap is that students have not properly understood the NEP. Or you could also say, NEP has not been properly explained to the students.

Learning is not just about passing a subject — it is about preparing for the real world. For example, when we teach Sole Trading Concern, the goal is not just to make every student a sole proprietor. The real purpose is to help students understand how a sole trader works, what responsibilities they have, and how that business structure operates. Similarly, when we teach Company Formation, it is not to suggest that every student must go out and start their own company. The aim is to help students understand how companies are structured, what policies they follow, their legal framework, and how management processes work.

The same principle applies to the NEP. The system is offering opportunities — but bridging the gap between what the system offers and what the student takes from it is entirely the student's responsibility.

Let me share a simple but beautiful example:

One day, I was speaking to my Guruji (mentor), from whom I have learned so much. I asked him, *"Sir, how do we know if a student has truly understood what we are teaching?"*

He gave a very insightful reply:

"Salim, when we teach, we always ask - 'Did you understand?" Every teacher asks this. And when a student replies, 'Yes, I understood,' at that very moment, the teacher's responsibility ends, and the student's responsibility begins."

Practical Implementation: Combine Learning with Experience

In today's world, practical implementation is essential. Whatever we are learning must be applied —otherwise, knowledge remains incomplete. For example, if you study advertisement campaigns in theory, it is not enough. You should try running a small advertisement campaign yourself, even on a small scale. Only then will you truly understand how it works. Students today must see Google, Artificial Intelligence, and other modern tools as their teachers too. The education system is evolving. Everywhere you hear about AI, Data Analytics, Digital Marketing —but are students practically applying these things? Are they experimenting with them?

Students must step beyond the classroom. Doing a part-time job does not just give you money —it gives you experience, which no textbook can teach. That is why students should actively seek to learn and gain experience in parallel with their education. Moreover, students should follow their passion while learning. Whether your passion is in computers, public speaking, marketing, content creation, entrepreneurship —pursue it actively alongside your studies. Passion-driven learning leads to deeper understanding and long-term success.

I have often seen students giving up on their passions. For example, someone may be an expert in accounting, but ends up taking a marketing job just for immediate employment — and slowly forgets their real talent. Remember —don't give up on your passion just because a job is not available right now. If you stay consistent, the right opportunity will come.

Let me share a real-life example:

One of my friends had a dream—he wanted to work in Dubai. One day, I asked him, *"What if you take a small job here in India for now?"* His reply was remarkable: *"Salim bhai, either I will work in Dubai, or I won't work at all. If I don't get a job in Dubai, I will wait—but I won't compromise."* Finally, after two and a half to three years, he got the job he wanted—and is now working successfully in Dubai.

You can call it stubbornness or strong determination—but his clarity of purpose and confidence led him to success. The truth is—no education system can give you passion. Passion comes from within. But if you combine education with real-world experience and follow your passion consistently, success will follow. Wasting time will not help. Students today need to change their method and style of learning—education must not be limited to theory. A powerful combination of learning and doing is what will make you truly industry-ready.

Interaction with Teachers: A Student's Responsibility

Building a connection with teachers is very important. Every teacher tries to explain things in different ways. And remember - every teacher is an institution in himself or herself.

I always give this example:

A teacher is like an ocean. Now it depends on what kind of vessel you bring.

If you bring a small cup, you will take away only a cupful of knowledge.

If you bring a bucket, you will take away a bucketful of knowledge.

It entirely depends on you — the more you are ready to take, the more you will receive.

I would also like to share a personal experience here. When I was a student, some of my teachers used to go out of their way to help me. I still remember my degree college teachers: Prof. Hysinta, Prof. Sarita, Sebastian Sir, Gafoor Sir, Father Solomon, Father Patrick, Magithia Sir, D'mello Sir, Jharna Miss, Miss Vinny Machado, Pitambar Patil Sir, Romamaulik Miss, D'mello Sir, Milind Sir and our Shaikh Sir (New English College — Vasai) . Each one of them was like an institution. They would go beyond the classroom to guide us.

The truth is — every teacher has a divine quality hidden within. You don't need to do much. You just need to take the first step and interact with them. The moment you take one step towards your teacher, they will take ten steps towards you. They will start recognizing you by name, they will understand your strengths and weaknesses — and that's when miracles start happening in your learning journey. Someone once told me, *"Sir, students don't attend college anymore. Attendance has become very low."* My answer was simple — one reason attendance is low is because there is no connection between students and teachers. If there is no connection, how will students develop interest in learning? That is why here too, the responsibility lies with the students. It is the student's responsibility to connect with their teachers. They should share their problems, ask questions, and seek solutions from their teachers. Teachers are ready to help — but students must take the initiative.

Education Should Be Vision-Driven, Not Semester-Driven

Students should not become semester—driven — they should become vision-driven. A student's target should not be limited to "JUST CLEARING SEMESTER 1" or "JUST PASSING SEMESTER 2". Instead, their target should be where they want to go in life - and how they will use education to get there.

For example:

If a student wants to become an entrepreneur, they should focus on learning entrepreneurial skills through their education.

If a student wants to work in a banking career, he or she should absorb banking knowledge from his or her education system.

If a student is interested in finance, he or she should learn finance deeply from the syllabus and beyond.

The key is that before selecting a course, students should first have clarity about their future goals.

If you want to start a business — what should you learn?

If you want to do a job — what should you train for?

If you want to work in another country — what extra preparation should you do?

If you want to pursue higher studies abroad — what should your plan be?

All of this requires planning. If a student makes the wrong choices in this planning stage, his or her entire career can go off track. That is why, during the 3 years of graduation, a student should take his or her education positively and seriously, and always keep his or her future vision clear.

A degree is not the end—it is a tool to build your future.

But what kind of future you build—depends on your vision.

Attendance: A Student's Responsibility

Whenever we talk about students, attendance naturally becomes an important discussion point. The real question is not whether the lectures are entertaining or not, or whether the lecture quality is high or low. The real question is this—it is the student's responsibility to attend the lectures.

Let me share an example.

I once taught at a small college where each class had around 70–80 students. There were three divisions - FY, SY, and

TY - so the total strength was about 250 students. But in reality, attendance was becoming very low. On most days, only about 100 students attended college. It was a small institution; many students were working part-time jobs, and some simply skipped classes. It had become difficult to manage. One day, a singing and dance competition was announced in the college. I noticed that only 1 or 2 students had signed up for participation. I went to the class and asked them why they were not participating. The students replied: *"Sir, we can dance, we can sing - but who will watch us? Hardly 50–100 students come to college. If only 10–20 of us perform, there will be no audience in the hall. Performing in an empty hall is no fun." Here, the issue was not about entertainment or passion - it was about the energy of performing in front of a crowd.*

I asked them one simple question:

"When one student performs on stage, how many friends usually come to watch? At least 5–7 friends, right?" So if 15–20 students participate, naturally each participant will bring his or her group to the audience. That alone would fill the hall. And that is exactly what happened. We eventually got 20–25 students to participate, and on the day of the event, around 200–220 students attended. The audience came. The energy was there.

This is the power of taking initiative. If one student decides to attend college, his or her friends also start attending. When friends start coming, their friends' friends also come - and gradually, the entire environment improves.

Attendance is ultimately the responsibility of the student. By taking that responsibility, students not only improve attendance but also create an atmosphere of learning, participation, and transformation within the college. Remember—change starts with you. One positive step from you can inspire many others.

Balancing Part - Time Work and Education: No Excuses, Only Effort

There are many students who work while they learn. They do part-time jobs and also pursue their education. But often, the first excuse from such students is: *"Sir, I do a job, so I can't attend college regularly.* I will attend only the minimum lectures." Here, I would like to share a real example of a student from my own experience. One of my distant relatives—my cousin's son—came to my college one day and said: *"Bhaijaan, I want to join college and complete my degree."*

Looking at this boy, my first thought was — this is going to be tough. I felt teaching him would be a big challenge, and since he was a family member, I couldn't take strict action against him either. But what surprised me was his passion for education and his excitement to complete his degree. He was working a part-time job and had to manage college alongside that. To my surprise — this boy started attending my 7:30 A.M. lecture every morning. Even though he used to work night shifts, he would still come to class with red, sleepy eyes — tired but determined. After attending the morning lecture, he would go home around noon to rest.

And the best part?

He completed his graduation with distinction!

This is what a true student looks like — one who doesn't make excuses, but delivers output. In my career, I have seen many such students — they work part-time, attend lectures, gain experience, and also complete their education successfully. They don't give excuses — they give results.

On the other hand, I've also seen students who constantly make excuses:

"Sir, I can't attend lectures because I'm doing a job."

I asked one such student:

"How much do you earn from your part-time job?"

He said: ₹10,000 to ₹15,000 per month.

"So, in a year?"

He replied: ₹1 lakh to ₹1.5 lakh.

Then I asked him another sharp question:

"The phone you are using — your iPhone — how much does it cost?"

He proudly said: ₹1 lakh.

Now think — is this student working just to maintain a lifestyle? To pay phone bills?

Here lies the difference:

Many students do part-time jobs only to fulfill their personal wants - and then they neglect education.

If that's the case, I would tell them honestly - *"Don't do the job. Stop using that phone. Focus on your studies first."* Commerce teaches you not just how to increase income, but also how to control expenses. When you reduce unnecessary expenses, your savings grow. So my request to students who are doing part-time jobs just to cover personal expenses: Don't sacrifice your education. Prioritize learning.

Now, there are students who truly need to work - because their families depend on them. For them, I remain silent because their situation is different. But even for them, my advice would be: Try to attend the maximum number of lectures possible - because to build a successful future, you need both experience AND education. Whether you want to become a future businessman or an excellent employee, both require a balance of learning and experience.

Target-Oriented Learning: Know What You Want and Learn What You Need

One real-life story that I always remember is about a student who had a very famous line. Whatever I suggested to him - whether it was solving extra problems or writing extra answers - his reply would always be the same: *"Sir, mujhe toh bas itna hi karna hai."* If I told him, *"Beta, solve a few extra Accounts problems,"* he would smile and say, *"Sir, mujhe toh bas itna hi karna hai."* If I suggested, *"Beta, write some extra answers in Economics - they will help you,"* again the same reply - *"Sir, mujhe toh bas itna hi karna hai."*

One day I finally asked him seriously, *"Beta, what do you mean by 'BAS ITNA HI KARNA HAI'?* Why do you always say this?" His answer was eye-opening. He said, *"Sir, my goal is to take over my father's dry fruit business. I know exactly what I need to learn for that. I focus on those subjects and skills that will help me grow the business. I learn regularly - but I don't waste time on things that won't help me in my future."* I was truly impressed. This is what we call target-oriented learning - when a student knows exactly what they want, and learns what is required for their goal. On the other hand, I have also seen many students who enter B.Com without any goal. They come to college simply because their friends come, or their boyfriend or girlfriend comes, or their group comes. Now, should we look at this as positive or negative? In one way, it is positive - at least it improves attendance. But if these students continue without any direction, it can easily become negative.

As a teacher, I always believe that even making friends, building relationships, forming groups - this is also part of education. It develops communication skills, teamwork, and social confidence. But here is the key difference:

A real degree is not just about books.

A real degree is about education, knowledge, communication skills, confidence, leadership, teamwork, creativity, problem-solving, involvement in events, participation in cultural activities - everything that shapes your personality.

If you simply sit at home and collect a certificate, it is only a piece of paper.

But when you actively engage in college life, when you connect with your teachers and peers, when you learn with purpose - that is when your degree becomes meaningful. Coming back to my student, was he wrong in saying *"mujhe toh bas itna hi karna hai"?* Not at all.

He had complete clarity. He came to college, he focused on the right subjects, and he gained practical experience from his family business. And today? He is a successful dry fruits exporter. Whenever he meets me, he laughs and says, **"Sir, mujhe toh bas itna hi karna tha - aur wahi kiya!"**

Have clarity. Know what you want. Learn what you need. And make sure your college life is an experience of true growth.

SPEAKUP: EXPRESS, DEBATE, AND PARTICIPATE

One very important point I want to highlight is that students should actively participate in debates, discussions, and conversations. They should freely express their likes, dislikes, opinions, and ideas. It is important for students to have a platform where they can speak their minds.

In our time, this was very difficult. Opportunities to speak openly in front of teachers and friends were very limited. But today, students have many more platforms — classroom discussions, college events, debate competitions, social clubs, and more. Unless a student speaks about what he or she feels, what he or she is passionate about, and what ideas he or she has — those thoughts will not grow. They will remain inside. But the more a student speaks, the more confident he or she becomes, and the more his or her thinking develops. Students should feel excited to come to college — excited to learn new things, to participate in events, to interact with teachers and peers, to express their ideas. This excitement is a key part of their growth. In fact, the responsibility of building this culture does not lie only with the education system, or only with teachers, or only with parents.

The biggest responsibility lies with the students themselves.

Students must understand this responsibility and accept it. They must take ownership of their own growth. If they stay silent, if they stay inactive, no one else can do the learning for them. College is a stage— but the student must be ready to step on it and perform.

The Stage is Yours. At the heart of this chapter lies one truth—graduation is not about marks; it is about transformation. Yes, teachers, parents, and the system play a role. But ultimately, your future is in your hands. Take responsibility. Participate. Connect. Apply your learning. Speak up. Build yourself. A certificate may help you get an interview. But your real skills, confidence, and personality will build your career.

As I always say:

"Take charge of your growth - because no one else can walk your journey for you."

And as my father used to say:

"If a person cannot help himself, no one in the world can help him."

Your growth, your transformation, your success - begin with YOU.

So dear students, remember this—if you keep waiting for the system, the teachers, or your parents to push you, you may end up graduating with a degree in one hand and an excuse in the other. And trust me, excuses don't get jobs or promotions! College life is not a rehearsal; it's the actual stage. Don't sit in the audience clapping for others—get up, walk on the stage, and own your script. Because no one ever became successful by just perfecting the art of bunking lectures or forwarding WhatsApp jokes. At the end of the day, your degree is just a piece of paper. But your effort, skills, and confidence—that's your real currency. And unlike paper, this currency never goes out of circulation.

Now, before you close this chapter thinking you've heard enough about student responsibility, let me warn you: the next chapter might just make you call your parents immediately (don't worry, this time not for pocket money!). Because what happens when students are ready but parents push the wrong buttons? Well, that's a comedy, a tragedy, and a family drama all rolled into one.

Flip the page… things are about to get even more interesting.

CHAPTER 7

THE SILENT CURRICULUM: PARENTING DURING COMMERCE EDUCATION

In earlier chapters, we explored how the education system, teachers, and students themselves shape a child's learning journey. But there is one influence that is even stronger—the role of parents. When a child clears CLASS 10, it is not just a student's milestone—it becomes a turning point for parents as well. At this stage, a parent's guidance can either open doors to true learning and vision, or unknowingly limit the child's future.

This chapter is a heartfelt message to parents, based on my 25 years of experience and real stories from my teaching journey. It is deeply connected to the core message of this book, **"Degree in Hand, Vision on Hold—Rethinking Commerce Education."** Because if parents do not rethink their role, we will continue to produce students with degrees, but without vision.

Parenting Before CLASS 10: A Journey, Not a Race for Marks

Parenting begins long before formal education. Even when a child is only a few days old, parents start making thoughtful decisions, starting with something as simple as choosing the child's name. They wonder, will it sound good? Will it suit the child? Will people pronounce it easily? These early decisions reflect the deep care and attention that parents naturally give. As the child grows, parents continue making small but important choices. They think about who will give the baby a massage, which oil is best, and which doctor to choose—one who gives strong medicines or one who prefers milder treatments. Every choice is made with love and a focus on the child's comfort. When the child begins exploring the world, parents proudly encourage their interests. If the child enjoys dancing, they enroll the child in a dance class. If the child hums songs around the house, they send the child for singing lessons. If the child watches martial arts or action cartoons, they happily enroll the child in karate or boxing.

I remember a conversation with one parent whose child loved to dance.

I asked, *"Have you noticed if your child is also drawn to the music itself?"*

The parent paused—they had never thought about it that way. This is how true parenting works—by observing what lies beneath the surface.

Until Class 10, most parents are happy to support their child's talents, whether big or small. But something strange often happens after Class 10. Suddenly, the focus shifts to just one thing: marks.

The CLASS 10 Result: A Turning Point for Parents

When CLASS 10 results are announced, the conversation in many homes shifts immediately toward stream selection: Science, Commerce, or Arts. Too often, this choice is made purely on the basis of marks, without considering the child's true interests or strengths. In my years of teaching, I have seen how this mindset can either help a child flourish or trap a child in the wrong path. I remember one student who scored just 45–50% in CLASS 10. The family was worried, unsure of what to do. Eventually, they enrolled him in Commerce. To everyone's surprise, he discovered a passion for Business Studies and Accounts. His confidence grew, and today, he is thriving in his chosen field. On the other hand, I saw another student who scored 75–80%. His parents proudly declared, **"He will do CA!"** But they never asked him whether he actually liked Accountancy or Commerce. The result was heartbreaking. The child struggled, lost confidence, and barely managed to pass his exams.

Marks alone do not define a child's interest or potential. Sometimes, even lenient checking or easy papers can inflate marks, leading to the wrong stream choice. As Albert Einstein wisely said, *"Everybody is a genius. But if you judge a fish by its ability to climb a tree, it will live its whole life believing it is stupid."* Parents must remember that they know their child far better than any mark sheet can show. The right stream should match the child's natural strengths, not just its percentage.

Choosing the Right Stream: Beyond Marks

After Class 10, it is natural for parents to focus on scores. But this is also the right time to ask deeper questions.

What does my child truly enjoy?

What are their strengths?

What sparks their curiosity?

Most students at this stage are not ready to decide their career alone. Many do not even know what careers are connected to Science, Commerce, or Arts. Only a few students have clear ideas, and it is perfectly normal for others to still be unsure. This is where parents must step in as guides, not as decision-makers. Career counseling, discussions with teachers, and open family conversations can help the child discover their path. Unfortunately, many average-scoring students are pushed into Commerce as a so-called "SAFE" option. But without interest, they lose motivation quickly. Like any stream, Commerce too requires passion and purpose. The decisions parents make today can shape their child's entire future.

The Science Student Story The Trap of Easy Choices

One real story that stays with me is about a student who struggled through two years of Science. Finally, his parents said, *"Science isn't working let's shift him to Commerce."* But was this truly the right choice? As I often say,

"If a child could not handle the grind of Science for two years,

How will they suddenly manage the demands of Commerce?"

If a child cannot manage Science, why not explore vocational courses, IT programs, or creative fields? Unfortunately, many parents move their children into Commerce simply because it appears easier. But this can lead to further struggles. The right path is not always the one that looks easy, but the one that matches the child's abilities and interests.

Is Commerce Really the "EASY OPTION"?

Many parents today view Commerce as a fallback option. If Science does not work out, or if Arts is seen as less promising, they opt for Commerce. But is this truly a wise choice? I often use a simple analogy. Imagine a busy Vadapav stall. It attracts a large crowd. But does a crowd always mean quality? Not necessarily. Similarly, Commerce has become a crowded stream today. Many parents select it just because it seems popular or easy. But the popularity of a stream does not guarantee that it is the right fit for every child. Choosing a stream based on trends or assumptions can lead to years of frustration. A stream should always be chosen after understanding what the child is passionate about and where their strengths lie.

The Hidden Free Time in Commerce: Who Fills It?

There is another important reality that parents often overlook. In Commerce education, students generally have more free time than in other streams like Science. At first, many parents feel relieved: *"At least my child is not under too much academic pressure."* But here lies a hidden question. If Commerce students have so much free time, what fills it? This time can either become an opportunity for positive learning, or it can easily drift toward distractions. Without proper guidance, students often fall into unhealthy routines during these years. This is where parents must stay involved and aware. They should know how their child is spending time after college hours.

Is the child using the time for personal development?

online learning?

reading, or projects?

Or is the child wasting time in endless social media scrolling or getting involved in unhealthy habits? Commerce education alone does not guide the child here. It is the parents who must take the lead.

The Influence of Peer Groups A Real Story

Peer groups have an even bigger role in shaping a student's mindset during these years. I have seen this clearly in my own teaching life. There was a group of Commerce students in my college who were very close friends. They did everything together: attending lectures, participating in college events, and also going on frequent outings. They had a wonderful sense of team spirit, and on the surface, everything looked very positive. But when the exam results were announced one semester, two students from this same group failed in a couple of subjects. I called them to my office and asked them gently, *"When your whole group passed, why did you two struggle?"*

Their answer revealed an untold side of commerce life. One student replied, *"Sir, both of us work part-time. We can't attend as many classes as the others. Our friends come from better-off families, so they can manage both studies and fun. We struggle to balance everything."* I asked, *"But when you go on outings with the group, how do you manage that?"* The student smiled and said, *"Sir, we take leave from work and lose our pay for those outings. But we couldn't take leave for exam preparation."* Even though their friends tried to help them catch up, these two students couldn't manage. The result was failure.

This taught me a **vital truth.** In today's Commerce education, peer groups often fill the gaps left by the system. A motivated and positive group can lift a student's thinking. But a mismatched group, even if well-meaning, can quietly derail someone's academic progress.

Friends Visiting Home The Parents' Silent Role

One of the most practical ways parents can stay connected to their child's journey is by observing their child's friends. Often, when friends visit the house, parents focus only on hospitality. But this is a valuable opportunity to quietly understand who the child is spending time with. Without being judgmental, parents should observe them.

How these friends talk,

What their mindset is,

What goals they discuss,

Are these friends encouraging personal growth, or promoting distractions?

Are they focused and balanced, or casual about academics and life?

This simple observation gives parents valuable insight into their child's environment. If parents sense danger signs—mismatched values, negative influence—they can then gently counsel their child to choose better circles. After all, friends have a deep impact on shaping a child's habits, thinking, and even vision. As the saying goes:

"Tell me who your friends are, and I will tell you who you are."

In Commerce education, where the system leaves plenty of unstructured time, the peer group often acts as an informal educator. That is why it is so important for parents to stay aware.

The Observation Effect   How Environment Shapes a Child

There is another story that highlights how much a child's environment shapes his or her thinking, even without formal teaching. I know a young man who does not work and has no active plans for his future. Yet, every evening, without fail, he meets five friends at a tea stall. Now here's the interesting part. These five friends are all successful in different areas of business   some in construction, others in property deals, some managing industrial contracts.

Every evening, this boy listens to their conversations. He hears things like,

"I closed this deal today,"

or **"I earned this commission,"**

or **"We started a new project."**

At the moment, he has no role in their businesses. He is simply an observer. But as a teacher and mentor, I know this much: it is only a matter of time before this boy tries to enter small construction or property deals himself whether or not he is ready. He is absorbing the environment, even unknowingly. This is what I call the Observation Effect. A child becomes what he or she hears, sees, and experiences every day. If the environment encourages growth and vision, the child moves forward. If it encourages shortcuts or casual thinking, the child's potential remains limited. In Commerce education, where formal learning often leaves practical gaps, the environment plays an even bigger role. Parents must understand that observation is also education.

Parenting with Respect, Not Fear

I must share another real experience from my teaching career. One day, I had to call the father of an irregular student to my office. The father arrived confidently and proudly said, *"Sir, my son fears me. Whatever I say, he obeys."* I smiled gently and asked,

If your son fears you so much,

why is he irregular in college?

Why does he skip classes ?

And why did he not tell you the truth when I called you here?

The father was taken aback. He had no answer. This is a mistake many parents make. They think that fear builds discipline. But fear only creates temporary obedience. It does not build responsibility. It does not create an open bond where the child can share doubts, worries, or mistakes.

If parents want their child to genuinely succeed, they must move beyond fear and build respect and trust. Building a

Bond of Trust. For a child to truly thrive, the parent-child relationship must be based on trust, not fear. A child should feel safe to say:

"Papa, I don't understand Commerce,"

or "Mummy, this stream is not right for me,"

or even, "I want to explore other options."

If a child lives in fear, he or she will suffer in silence. He or she will continue down the wrong path simply because he or she is too afraid to speak up. On the other hand, when a child feels safe at home, he or she can face the world with courage. He or she can ask for help, admit when he or she is confused, and seek better paths. And that is exactly the kind of future we should want for our children. A child who feels safe, respected, and loved at home will grow into a confident learner and an individual with vision. Isn't that the true goal of education?

Recognizing Business Potential A Key Role for Parents

There is one more important role for parents in commerce education that we have not yet discussed in this chapter. Parents must learn to observe their child during these three years of college, and recognize whether the child shows signs of business potential. Every child has different strengths. It is important for parents to honestly judge:

Does my child show risk-taking ability?

Does my child have the courage to speak in public?

Does my child confidently make decisions without hesitation?

Does my child stand firm when he or she believes in something?

If you see such qualities in your child, remember they have the potential to become a businessman or an entrepreneur. Sadly, many parents unknowingly discourage this. They focus only on safe zones and traditional thinking, pushing the child toward a secure job. I would like to share a lesson from.

My Guru, who has deeply influenced my thinking, used to say:

"A farmer earns twice a year, because he harvests two crops.

An employee earns 12 times a yearbecause they get a salary every month.

But a businessman earns 365 times a year because every day is an opportunity.

Parents should not fear the idea of their child becoming a businessman. They should not limit the child's thinking to employee roles alone. If your child works as an employee, they will take care of their own family. But if they become a businessman, they can take care of many families—their own, and those of their employees and community. When we look at the stories of great entrepreneurs, we always find that the role of parents was critical. Somewhere along the way, the parents gave freedom, support, and confidence to help their child think big. If our education system sometimes fails to produce entrepreneurs after commerce education, parents too share some responsibility. If the home environment does not allow freedom, innovation, healthy debate, exposure to new experiences—the child will hesitate to think like an entrepreneur. That is why, in true parenting, there should be freedom, encouragement for innovation, open debates, shared experiences, and meaningful conversations between parent and child. Only then will commerce education truly produce entrepreneurial thinkers.

Parents not only have to notice their child's potential but also learn to handle a new phase of parenting—when children begin to question everything. This stage often feels uncomfortable, but in reality, it is a hidden blessing.

When Children Start Questioning Parents…

A few years ago, a parent walked into my office looking half-frustrated and half-defeated. He sighed and said, *"Sir, I don't understand what's happening. My son has suddenly started questioning everything. Earlier, he used to agree with us on every decision. But now, every single thing becomes an argument! We told him we'll buy him a bike. Instead of being happy, he gave us a full research report—ten different brands, engine comparisons, mileage details, YouTube reviews—and at the end declared, 'Only this model will work for me!' Who gave him this much confidence?"*

I laughed and replied, **"Education did!"**

Because let's be honest—till Class 10, children mostly nod their heads like obedient dolls. But once they cross that stage, something magical (and to parents, sometimes tragical) happens: they start asking questions. Parents say, *"Beta, wear this shirt, it looks good." Child replies, "No, I like oversized T-shirts. This is out of fashion." Parents say, "Eat your vegetables." Child replies, "Why? Green veggies don't have enough protein. I need more eggs." Parents say, "This phone is best for you." Child replies, "Papa, this model doesn't even have AMOLED display? How will I survive in 2025 with LCD?" You see, what parents call "argument," education calls "thinking." What parents call "zid," I call "mindset opening."*

A Proud Moment in Disguise

Dear parents, let me tell you one truth: You should worry when your child stops asking questions, not when he starts. A silent child is not necessarily an obedient child—sometimes, it means he has stopped engaging. But if he's debating with you, challenging you, even bargaining like a mini-lawyer, it means his brain is active. Think about it: if your child can argue with you at home, he can argue with the world outside. If he can question your decisions, he can question wrong practices in society. If he can confidently say, *"Papa, this bike is better than that one,"* tomorrow he might say, *"Boss, this business model is better than your outdated one."* Isn't that what we secretly want—a confident, independent thinker?

Respect vs. Opinion

Now, I know what you are thinking: *"But sir, he doesn't respect me anymore. He just keeps arguing."*

No, my dear parent. Respect and opinion are two different things. Just because your child is presenting his opinion, doesn't mean he has lost respect. It simply means he has developed a voice. And trust me, that voice is precious. If he's questioning you, it means he's learning to question the world. If he's presenting logic at home, it means he will present logic tomorrow in his office, in his business, in his life. And isn't that a proud moment for you?

Parent–Child Comedy Show

Let me end with a hilarious truth. Parents: *"Beta, go and study!"* Child: *"Why? Didn't Einstein say imagination is more important than knowledge?"* Parents: *"We didn't talk like this to our parents."*

Child: *"Exactly. That's why we are talking like this now!"* Yes, sometimes it feels like children are running a full-blown debate competition at home. But instead of shutting them down, sit with them, argue with them, even lose sometimes. Because the day you win every argument, your child might stop trying. And the day he stops trying, education has lost its purpose. So next time your child argues with you, don't get angry. Smile, pour yourself a cup of tea, and think: *"Good! At least my child is not a robot. He's a thinker. He's learning not just to follow, but to lead."*

If we want to move from a **"DEGREE IN HAND"** to a **"VISION IN HEART,"** this change must begin at home

Why Parents Must Stay Involved During Commerce Education

This brings us to a deeper question about the role of parenting. If we think about it, from the moment a child is born, parents are deeply involved. They carefully choose the child's name, the doctor, the medicine, the diet. Every small decision is guided by love and observation. But after the Class 10 result, something changes. Parents become more focused on marks, streams, and admissions. The child moves into junior college—11th and 12th— which is still more of an extension of school life. Then the child enters the three-year Commerce degree program. Now here is where many parents unknowingly step back. They assume that since the child is in college, the teachers and education system will take care of everything.

But let us reflect. Just as parents once proudly noticed a child's dance steps and thought *"maybe they will become a dancer,"* or noticed their singing and thought *"maybe a singer,"* shouldn't they now observe what kind of thinker their child is becoming during these three years of Commerce education?

More importantly, parents should try to identify their child's potential direction during this period. If the child shows signs of entrepreneurial thinking — such as risk-taking ability, leadership qualities, decision-making confidence, or creativity — parents should recognize this and encourage it. On the other hand, if the child is more inclined toward employment, parents should not settle for a general thought like, *"Any job will do."* They should carefully observe what type of job would truly fit their child's abilities and interests.

Does the child show a natural interest and skill in marketing — perhaps they enjoy communication, promotion, or branding? Is the child more comfortable with accounting or financial work — do they have a strong grasp of numbers, analysis, and financial systems? Or does the child show interest in other financial activities — like stock markets, banking, fintech, or e-commerce?

These observations can help parents guide their child toward a career path that matches their strengths. One of the major reasons why students with a **"DEGREE IN**

HAND" often end up with **"VISION ON HOLD"** is that no one, not even their parents, helped them clearly identify what they were truly good at — and what direction would best suit them. This is why colleges too should support parents during these three years. It is not enough to educate only the students. Regular circulars, orientation sessions, and open communication with parents can help them understand what qualities to look for, what questions to ask, and how to support their child's career decisions.

Without this partnership between the education system and the home, it will remain difficult to create true entrepreneurs and visionary professionals through Commerce education. However, if parents and educators work together, the possibilities are endless.

Throughout this book, we have explored how Commerce education today needs a major rethink. In earlier chapters, we saw how the system often leaves students with theoretical knowledge but little practical clarity. We also saw how peer groups, teachers, and the changing business world all influence a child's growth. But one factor remains constant— the influence of parents. If parents actively observe, guide, and support their child during these crucial three years of Commerce education, they can help turn a simple degree into a real career vision. Without this support, too many students graduate with a degree in hand, but their vision is still on hold.

One real-life story always inspires me.

Do you know that Ratan Tata, one of India's most respected business leaders, was raised by his grandmother after his parents separated? His grandmother encouraged him to think independently, follow his passion, and never fear taking bold decisions. This parenting style shaped his values—and helped him later build one of India's greatest business empires. Without this early encouragement, perhaps even a brilliant mind like Ratan Tata's could have remained "ON HOLD."

Parents must remember: A child's vision is not built in the classroom alone. It is built at home. In today's Commerce education, where the system often lacks entrepreneurial guidance, parental involvement is more important than ever. When parents and educators work together, Commerce education can truly evolve. Then we will not only produce students with degrees—we will produce young people with vision, confidence, and the courage to create their own path. It is time for all of us—parents, teachers, and society—to help our children light that flame.

So parents, remember this: if you keep treating your child like a robot, don't be shocked when they grow up and say, *"System error: vision not found!"* Parenting in commerce is not about forcing your child into CA just because Sharmaji's son cleared it. If marks alone decided success, half the comedians in India would still be accountants today! Your role is simple: don't just pay their college fees, pay attention to their dreams. Because one good conversation at home can save three years of confusion in college. And now, before you pat yourself on the back for being a *"responsible parent,"* let me tell you: our next chapter will hit even harder. It's about mindsets—the invisible software running in every student's head. The question is, will it build a nation… or just build another queue outside job interviews?

CHAPTER 8

DEGREES DON'T BUILD NATIONS, BUT MINDSETS DO

Learning to Lead, Not Just to Follow

In the journey so far through this book, we've explored how students are often driven by marks, moulded by teachers, directed by parents, and limited by a system that rarely asks: What does the student truly want to become? We've questioned whether commerce education today creates thinkers or task-doers, dreamers or duty-bearers. We've seen how degrees are handed out, yet visions are still held back because the spark of entrepreneurship is missing. Now, let us shift our attention to a bold and timely development: the New Education Policy (NEP) 2020. While it arrives as a promising wind of change, the big question is: Is it changing the mindset, or just the methods? And more importantly, Is it preparing students to create jobs, or only to get them?

NEP 2020 – A Good Start, But Still Not Enough

When we read the New Education Policy 2020, we feel that it is a very thoughtful step taken by the government to improve our education system. There are many positive changes in it, like flexibility in learning, skill development, and a focus on overall growth. But after going through the policy and connecting it with what we see in real life, one important thing feels missing: the business mindset. Even though the policy brings new methods, the direction is still the same: to prepare students for jobs, not for creating jobs.

If you have read my earlier chapters, you will remember that I shared how a businessman's child usually becomes a businessman. This is not because of any magic. It is simply because of the environment that builds the child's mindset. From childhood, such children see their parents taking risks, managing business challenges, buying assets, applying for loans, and growing their income. These children don't just hear about business — they see it happening around them every day. Slowly, they build a mindset: *"This is what I will do in the future."* So when the time comes to take a loan or make a business deal, it is not a new experience for them. They have already seen it many times. The only difference is, earlier they were watching it, now they are doing it. This kind of mindset needs to be built in all students. The New Education Policy should help students understand how to take risks, how to create something new, and how to make their ideas work in real life. But unfortunately, the policy doesn't succeed in building this business mindset. It teaches concepts, but not confidence. It gives theory, but not exposure.

I want to share some real-life examples.

One of my students came from a business family. One day, I told him, *"Why don't you apply to a good company? You will get a job easily with a salary of ₹40,000 to ₹50,000."* His reply shocked me, but it also made me proud. He said, *"Sir, I am planning to start a company where I will give ₹40,000 to ₹50,000 as salary to others."* That's the mindset. He was not talking about taking a job. He was talking about giving jobs. And this mindset didn't come from any classroom. It came from his home, from what he saw growing up. Now let me share another example:

One of my students came from a family where no one had ever done business. I once told him, *"Why don't you invest ₹1 or ₹2 lakh and start a small business? You can easily earn ₹40,000 to ₹50,000 per month."* His reply was also shocking, but for a different reason. He said, *"Sir, there is too much competition. A new business cannot survive easily. Who will take the risk of losing ₹2 lakhs? I'd rather do a job, take weekends off, earn ₹40,000 per month, and live peacefully. After all, we all have to die one day."* This is a completely different mindset. This student is not ready to take a chance. He is not wrong — he has simply never seen business happening around him. No one ever taught him that failure can be a learning step too.

So here lies the gap. Students from business families have a mindset that says, *"I can build something."* But students from non-business backgrounds are taught to play safe, to stay within limits, and not to take chances. The New Education Policy must understand these two mindsets and help both kinds of students. Those who want to do a job should get the right career guidance. But those who want to become entrepreneurs should get the tools, support, and mindset to start something of their own.

The policy should include practical learning on how to take a loan, how to repay it, how to plan a business, how to deal with failure, and how to grow slowly and wisely. It should not only teach students what business is, but also show them how to think like a businessperson. Until this happens, we will keep creating employees. But to build a strong India, we must create employers.

NEP 2020 is a beautiful initiative, and we must respect it. But no matter how beautiful a vehicle is, if the direction is wrong, we will not reach the right destination. The direction of education should now move towards mindset-building, not just syllabus-completing. We need students who are job-ready, yes — but also students who are startup-ready, risk-ready, and future-ready.

I remember one day, after a lecture, one of my students came to me and asked a very simple but powerful question. He said, *"Sir, you always say business is a great thing. You talk about growth, innovation, risk-taking, and success in entrepreneurship. Then why doesn't the education system help students like us who want to do business? If you already know from our results and classroom performance that we have the potential to become entrepreneurs, then why not start a business for us? Why don't you people give us a startup instead of a certificate?"*

This question really stayed with me. It was not a complaint — it was a reflection of what our education system is still missing. Why can't the education system itself identify potential entrepreneurs? If a student shows the right mindset, good performance, creativity, and practical thinking, why can't we support him or her with an initial business investment?

When the government is already giving funds to startups, when there are schemes to promote employment, and when crores are spent on job creation — then why not create a new scheme inside the education system itself? A scheme that says:

"If we can see a businessman in you, we will help you become one."

This can be merit-based and mindset-based. It can be given to those students who prove through their performance that they are not just learning for marks, but they are thinking beyond jobs. This can be a revolutionary step in the NEP framework. Let education not only end with a degree. Let it begin with a dream. And let that dream be backed not only by encouragement, but also by real investment.

Sometimes, it feels like our students are actually our best teachers. What I am writing here is not just my own observation—it is the story of my students. I may be using the pen and paper, but the ideas, the thoughts, the questions—everything belongs to them. They are the real authors behind this chapter.

Let me share one more real-life example.

One day, a student of mine came running to me and said, *"Sir, today I learned how to invest. I just invested ₹50,000 in the stock market."* I was shocked. I asked him, *"₹50,000? Where did you get that kind of money to invest?"* He looked at me and started laughing. He said, *"Sir, don't worry! There's an app where we get ₹50,000 to ₹1 lakh as virtual money, not real cash. It's just for learning. We buy and sell stocks and get to understand how investments work. It's not actual money. It's a simulation. You should also try it. Go online, register, and start investing. It teaches you how to invest without actually spending any money."* That moment stayed with me. I wasn't surprised at the app. I was surprised at how confidently a student had taken the first step toward understanding money, not in theory, but through practice.

Now just think, if our technology has reached a stage where students can learn stock trading without spending a single rupee, then why can't our education system do something similar for business learning? What if the New Education Policy introduced such business simulation apps, startup games, and investment challenges as part of daily education? What if students could play business today, and build businesses tomorrow? This is the kind of practical exposure that can turn interest into ambition. Today's young minds are ready. They don't need memorization. They need experiences. And if learning becomes exciting like a game, then someday, life will become their playing field, and business their winning strategy.

Sometimes, the most meaningful conversations happen outside the classroom. One evening, I was sitting casually with a student, and we were discussing various topics. Suddenly, he asked me,

"Sir, what exactly is innovation in business?"

It was a genuine question, asked with curiosity, not from a textbook, but from the heart. I paused for a moment and decided to share something personal instead of giving a standard definition. I told him about a memory from my childhood. *"Many years ago,"* I began, *"I was traveling with my father on a train from Vasai to Bombay. I must have been very young. That day, for the first time in my life, I saw water being sold in a bottle."* The student looked confused. *"I turned to my father and asked, 'What is this?' He smiled and said, 'It's bottled water. People buy it and drink it.' I was shocked. Coming from Vasai, a place where we say there's a fresh-water well in every home, the idea of buying water felt strange. In our locality, water was always free, sweet, and available. We never imagined it could ever become a product."* I paused and looked at the student. *"And yet today, bottled water is sold everywhere. Even in Vasai. Even in places full of water. This,"* I said to him, *"is innovation. Someone, somewhere, looked at something ordinary—like water and thought, 'Can I sell this?' And they did. That's what innovation means. Seeing opportunity where others see nothing."* He nodded slowly, processing what I'd said. But then came his reply, one that really made me think.

He said,

"Sir, in that case, all the great innovations have already been done. What is left for us? What can we now innovate?"

His words were simple, but deep. And they made me reflect on today's generation of students. They are not short of talent or intelligence. But somewhere, they feel the world has already moved ahead without them. That there's nothing new left for them to create. That they have missed the innovation bus. This is where our education system must step in. We must not just teach innovation—we must inspire it. We must show students that innovation doesn't always mean inventing something entirely new. Sometimes, it means improving what already exists. Sometimes, it means applying an old idea in a new way. And sometimes, it simply means asking a better question.

NEP 2020 must help students see that innovation is not finished—it is just beginning. The world is changing fast, and there will always be room for fresh ideas, smarter solutions, and new ways to solve age-old problems. Our students need to believe this. They need to feel that their ideas matter. Their thoughts count. Their future can be built, not borrowed. And that belief—that spark of possibility—can be the greatest innovation education ever brings. Sometimes, we meet students who don't just learn from us—they reflect what we ourselves have forgotten. This story is not from my college classroom, but from my coaching classes. One day, a student walked up to me, not with a question, but with a proposal. With complete confidence, he said,

"Sir, I want to form a partnership with you."

I was surprised. This was a student I was still teaching—he hadn't even completed his degree. And yet, here he was, asking to become my business partner. I smiled and asked him gently, *"What exactly do you want to do? Do you want to teach? Or do you want to run a business?"*

His answer made me pause.

"Sir, I want to do both. I want to teach like you, and I also want to run a business like you."

There was no confusion in his voice. There was no fear in his eyes. He had already decided. While most students at his age are busy collecting notes, figuring out which exam to clear next, and rushing to complete assignments, this student had already found his direction. That day, I explained to him the realities. I said, *"Teaching needs experience. A class needs investment. There's a lot more to it than passion."* I tried to shift his focus back to studies. He listened, he understood, and he quietly went back. But that wasn't the end of the story.

Years later, that same student became a teacher. He was not just a teacher, but a brilliant one. Today, he trains M.Com, B.Com, MBA students, and even prepares students for NET and SET exams. He didn't stop at getting a degree. He chose a mission. This is what I want to say to the education system. Many students today are not lazy. They are not directionless. But they are living a life without a clear goal. Their only mission is to complete a degree. But a degree is not a mission. It is just a milestone. What students really need is vision. A sense of purpose. A roadmap for life. Whether it is a job or a business, teaching or entrepreneurship, they should know where they are going and why. This is where the New Education Policy must play a bigger role. It should not just guide students on how to study, but also help them discover what they want to become. It should not only offer subjects—it should offer students a reason to wake up each morning with purpose. Let education not end in a mark sheet. Let it begin with a mission. Because the real result of education is not seen in exams, it is seen in the life a student builds after school is over.

A New Ray of Hope, But Only If Taken Seriously

When the New Education Policy (NEP) 2020 was announced, it felt like a fresh breath in a stale room. For the first time in many years, the education system was not just talking about exams and degrees—it was talking about skills, creativity, flexibility, and making students future-ready. NEP gave us a beautiful vision: a system where learning is joyful, meaningful, and connected to real life. It gave students the freedom to choose, the chance to explore, and the space to grow. It gave teachers the power to focus on understanding, not just on completing the syllabus. It gave parents the hope that their children would not just become degree-holders, but confident, capable individuals. But this vision remains a dream if we don't act. A good policy can bring change only when it moves beyond paper and enters the classroom. Right now, NEP sounds great in seminars, brochures, and presentations—but many students and teachers are still unaware of what it actually means. That's the problem. NEP is hope. But hope without action becomes disappointment. Imagine if NEP was fully implemented. What if a child in a remote village learns every subject in her mother tongue until Class 5? She would finally understand what she's learning. She wouldn't just copy answers and forget them the next day. She would ask questions, participate in class, and slowly gain the confidence that learning is meant for her too. Today, many rural students fall behind only because they don't understand the language of the textbook. NEP wants to solve that—but unless we train teachers and provide materials in regional languages, the idea will never reach the student. What if a 12-year-old boy learns coding as part of his school timetable? He builds a basic app to solve a local problem—maybe an app to track water supply or inform the nearest shopkeeper about delivery delays. His app may be simple, but the confidence it gives him will be powerful. He would stop seeing himself as *"just a student"* and start seeing himself as a creator. NEP supports such learning—but only a few private schools have adopted it. Government schools are still struggling with blackboards, let alone code. Now think about a teenager who loves both numbers and music. Under the old system, he had to pick only commerce or arts—not both. But NEP allows him to take Accountancy and Music together. That means he can dream of opening his own music school and managing its finances on his own. He doesn't have to give up one passion to follow another. NEP makes that possible—but how many colleges are actually allowing such combinations? Are we guiding students to design their own path, or still forcing them to follow old roadmaps?

Another powerful change NEP promises is to focus on communication and personality development. What if every student were trained to speak with confidence, face interviews, participate in debates, and present their ideas in class regularly? The fear of public speaking would go away. The student who was once shy would become a future leader. Isn't that the real purpose of education? Not just to remember formulas, but to express ideas. Sadly, many colleges still believe stage events are a waste of time. They want to *"complete the syllabus"* but forget to complete the student. NEP has the power to change all this. But a policy, no matter how brilliant, is useless if it's not implemented properly. In many places, schools and colleges have started using NEP as a fancy word to show progress, without making any real changes inside the classroom. Teachers are not trained in the new format. Students are not aware of their options.

Even parents are confused about what this policy means for their child's future. In short, NEP is moving forward in some places, but standing still in many others. If we truly want NEP to work, we must take it seriously. It should not be treated as a decorative idea, but as a system that requires discipline, planning, and accountability. Schools must be checked, not for how good their banners look, but for how well their students are learning. Teachers must be given the tools and training they need to teach creatively. Students must be told that education is no longer about mugging up answers, but about building their minds and skills. And most importantly, rural and small-town schools must be included in this change. If NEP only reaches metro cities, it will fail in its true mission. The New Education Policy is not just another reform. It is a lifeline. It is a chance to save an entire generation from becoming degree-holders without direction. But this chance will slip away if we keep delaying. We don't need another policy. We already have a good one. What we need is strict, honest, and urgent implementation. Let's not forget: India doesn't just need educated children. India needs empowered learners. And for that, we don't need another speech. We need action.

So here we are collecting degrees like trophies, but forgetting that nations are not built on framed papers; they are built on framed mindsets. A degree may open a door, but only the right mindset decides whether you walk in like a guest, an employee, or the owner. The truth is simple: education without mindset is like Wi-Fi without data; it looks connected, but nothing loads. And sadly, many of our graduates are still buffering. If mindsets are the real builders of nations, then who is shaping them? Spoiler alert: it's not the syllabus, not the exams, and definitely not the PowerPoint slides. Which means, it's time to hand the mic to the ones standing in the middle of this chaos every single day — the teachers. Because when commerce teachers stop teaching theory and start speaking reality, things get funny, fiery, and frighteningly true.

So turn the page. The staffroom door is about to open, and trust me, you've never heard teachers like this before.

CHAPTER 9

COMMERCE TEACHERS SPEAK ENOUGH THEORY, LET'S TALK REALITY

"What Happens When Teachers Remove the Filter?"

After spending chapters dissecting the chaos called commerce education, from confused students and cautious parents to overworked teachers and outdated policies, it was time to flip the mic. What do the teachers really think? Not the staffroom small talk. Not the scripted seminar lines. We're talking raw, honest, tea-sipping truth. So we asked them direct questions. No syllabus. No moderation. Just one-on-one. And guess what? The answers came in like a monsoon, equal parts thunder, lightning, and the occasional rainbow. Some teachers dropped gold: *"Make students pitch real businesses."* Others gave reality slaps: *"They don't know what a godown looks like!"* A few threw punches at the syllabus. One even suggested giving students ₹500 and letting them feel what it's like to lose money before they try to earn it. From witty one-liners to deep wisdom, from sarcasm to soul-searching, you're about to read what happens when the blackboard takes a backseat and the real voice of commerce education finally gets a chance to speak

"We Teach Business, But Do We Build Businessmen?"

Let's start with a question that sounds serious but can also make you laugh if you've spent enough time in the education system: Can today's commerce education actually prepare students to start their own business? You'd expect a confident "YES" from most teachers, right? After all, we teach Business Studies, Entrepreneurship, Marketing, and even throw in a little "LEADERSHIP SKILLS" here and there. But when we asked college teachers this very question, their answers came wrapped in caution tape. Just 17% said yes, a brave 11% said no, and the remaining 72% played it safe with a humble "PARTIALLY." In short, the system teaches business like we teach swimming—with no water in the pool. Now let's decode what "PARTIALLY" actually means. In the Indian education dictionary, "PARTIALLY" often means *"I'm saying yes because I don't want to say no, but please read between the lines."* It's the academic version of *"I like your idea, but…"* The teachers weren't wrong. Yes, we do teach about businesses, but we do it in PowerPoint slides, not in practice. Students know how to define an entrepreneur, but most have never met one. They can prepare a detailed project report for a fake startup in TYBCom, but panic when asked to sell even a packet of handmade rakhi in real life.

Let's be honest — our classrooms are like diet samosas. They look heavy on the outside, full of "IMPORTANT" subjects like

Business Law and Financial Accounting, but inside? There's no spice. No masala. Just dry theory wrapped in attendance sheets. Students write assignments on how Amazon changed the world but never learn how to build a basic website for their own idea. They memorize how Flipkart started in a garage but are never asked what business they could start from their own bedroom. We're basically producing YouTubers who never upload a video. If commerce education really worked the way it claims, half our chaiwalas would be running unicorn startups by now — because our students know how to price, promote, and profit… on paper. But in reality, they're scared to take even a ₹100 risk without asking *"Sir, is this in syllabus?"* We've created a breed of business thinkers who are excellent at presentations but terrified of execution. And you know what's worse? We've convinced them that this is normal. We hand them degrees in "COMMERCE" and hope the universe sends them "COMMON SENSE." The problem is not just the syllabus — it's the mindset we're breeding. We train students to believe that entrepreneurship is for the brave few, the lucky ones, the outliers. We forget to tell them: *"You can be that person too."* We celebrate job placements like Olympic medals, but treat startup ideas like distractions. A student who says *"I want to start something"* is gently told, *"First get a job, beta. Then think about passion."* By the time "THEN" comes, the passion is buried under EMIs and LinkedIn updates.

So what do we need? Not a revolution — just a little common sense with courage. Start with small changes: Let students run mini-businesses in college. Make "PITCH PRESENTATIONS" part of their exams. Replace one Viva with a real sale. Let them experience what it feels like to lose ₹50 of their own money — and learn ten times more from that loss than from ten definitions. And most importantly, let teachers stop being content deliverers and start being possibility generators. In conclusion — and yes, this one deserves a standing ovation — commerce education must stop preparing students only for PowerPoint and start preparing them for the Power of Practice. Until then, we'll continue to produce students who know the meaning of "ENTREPRENEUR," but never hear someone say, *"Why not you?"* And maybe, just maybe, that one line could change everything.

What one change would you suggest in commerce syllabus to help students think like entrepreneurs?

When we asked teachers what one change could help commerce students think like entrepreneurs, we didn't get textbook answers. We got reality checks — sharp, witty, and refreshingly honest. It turns out, the real solution isn't buried in the curriculum… it's buried under project files, outdated chapters, and "SAFE" teaching methods. The most common suggestion? *"Stop training students just to pass. Start training them to pitch."* Teachers are tired of students submitting 20-page reports on imaginary businesses while struggling to sell a single handmade bookmark. One teacher said it perfectly: *"Replace that TYBCom project with a real startup model. Let them pitch an idea. Let them fail. At least that failure will teach them more than full marks ever could."*

Some educators want to take it further with a subject called Startup Simulation where students ideate, build, and pitch real businesses. It sounds fancy, but the idea is simple: instead of only reading about Flipkart, let them create "TRIPCART" and test their own logistics model even if it's just delivering dabbas across the college campus. And then came the most entertaining (and brilliant) proposal: give students seed money ₹500 to be precise. Day one, they form teams. Day three, they're co-founders. Day seven, they're arguing over profits. And by day ten, the business is dead, but the learning? Unforgettable. That ₹100 loss will teach them what no 100-mark paper ever could.

Another recurring idea was: teach market trends that actually exist. While the syllabus is still discussing radio ads and direct selling, students are binge-watching D2C brands on Instagram and YouTube. One teacher joked, *"By the time our syllabus catches up with the market, the market has already moved to the Metaverse."* And he's not wrong.

But the most underrated gem of all? Reduce class size. Yes, it sounds simple. But imagine being an average student stuck in Row 11, behind three tall heads, next to a snoring friend, trying to listen to a soft-spoken teacher battling with a ceiling fan. Entrepreneurship requires confidence, and confidence starts with being seen and heard not hidden in a human jungle of roll numbers.

Other teachers called for field visits, real entrepreneur talks, on-the-job training, better business English, and earlier exposure to management studies. One even said, *"Stop only teaching Steve Jobs. Start introducing them to 'Vada-wala Shyamlal.' He built a business without Wi-Fi or a website."* Frankly, Shyam deserves to be in the syllabus.

If we truly want our commerce students to think like entrepreneurs, we need to stop preparing them to write answers and start preparing them to ask questions.

Let classrooms become launchpads.

Let projects become pitches.

Let failures become part of the curriculum.

Because no student ever became a businessperson just by learning definitions. They became one by daring to try even if it started with a ₹500 flop and a friend who forgot the stock. Change the method, and you might just change the mindset. And from there, everything else can begin.

Should practical business training (internships, live projects) be added more in commerce education? Why?

Imagine teaching swimming without ever entering a pool. That's how commerce education feels today—full of theory, but no depth. And when we asked teachers whether internships and live projects should be added more in commerce education, the answers were loud, clear, and slightly frustrated: *"Yes, and it's long overdue."*

One teacher put it bluntly: *"We are producing students who can draw the organizational chart of a company but don't know how an actual office looks."* Another one said, *"They know what a sales pitch is—but have never had to convince even one customer in real life."* That's the reality. Students are learning about markets without ever stepping into one. They write about inventory but have never stepped into a godown. They solve case studies, but have never seen how real businesses make decisions under pressure. Internships bring that missing piece. They're not just about making students "JOB-READY." They are about making students reality-ready. A student who spends even two weeks in a business setup learns how to communicate, how to coordinate, and more importantly—how to behave in a professional setting. No exam can teach that.

One teacher gave a brilliant example: *"Let them spend a week in a small printing press or courier service. They'll learn deadlines, delays, and diplomacy all at once."* And it's true. That noisy, sweaty office will teach them more about time management than any motivational poster ever can.

Some teachers even admitted the challenge of finding enough internships for the volume of commerce students. But that's no excuse. Even mini-projects, business model assignments, street-selling activities, or shadowing a local entrepreneur for a day can build real skills. *"Better they struggle in a project now than in a job later,"* said another faculty member wisely. And let's not forget the mindset shift. When students go out into the real world, they begin to ask better questions. Instead of just mugging up marketing concepts, they start thinking: Why do customers prefer brand A over brand B? What makes this shop busier than the one next door? That's where real commerce begins—not in notes, but in noticing. Today's students are full of ideas. They're building followers online, doing freelance gigs, and selling handmade stuff on Instagram. But our classroom is still stuck in blackboard mode. We need to meet them where they already are—in the real, messy, challenging world of business.

A student who only learns theory will only remember answers. But a student who gets to try, to fail, to fix, and to improve will remember how learning actually works. Let's stop acting like real business is something that starts after college. Let's help students start living it while they're still inside. Because no matter how good a syllabus looks on paper—it means nothing if it can't prepare students for a world that doesn't come with model answers.

Do you feel subjects like digital marketing and business finance should be compulsory for all commerce students? Why?

imagine a student today—sharp, smart, and glued to their phone. They can run a meme page, sell pre-loved jeans on Instagram, and make reels that hit 10K views overnight. But ask them how to price that product properly or how much profit they made—and silence. That's exactly why most teachers we spoke to said yes: Digital Marketing and Business Finance must be part of the core syllabus for all commerce students. Today's businesses are not born in boardrooms; they're born in browsers. Whether you're opening a chai stall or launching a fashion line, your first customer probably meets you online. That's where digital marketing becomes less of a subject and more of a survival instinct. One teacher said, *"It's the new language of business, and we're still teaching like it's 1999."*

Business Finance, on the other hand, is like brushing your teeth. You don't need to be an expert in dentistry, but you better know the basics or it's going to hurt. As one teacher pointed out: *"Most students think finance only matters when you're rich. They need to realize that finance is what helps you get there in the first place."*

Many teachers highlighted how students today think of starting their own businesses but don't understand credit, cash flow, or what EMI really means.

One teacher laughed and said, **"They think budget means shopping during sale season. It's time they learn what real budgeting looks like."**

Now some teachers did say—maybe not full-length deep dive for everyone, but at least a compulsory basic course in both subjects should be mandatory. Why? Because in today's job market, even if you're applying for a basic job—chances are, they'll ask you if you know Excel, social media basics, or how to read a sales report. And you can't answer with *"Sir, I topped in Theory of Cooperation."* Also, these subjects are immediately usable. Students can use digital marketing to grow their freelancing, sell t-shirts, promote a college fest, or build their personal brand. And business finance? That's useful the day they start earning—to budget, invest, avoid bad loans, and maybe finally understand that "0% EMI" is not as friendly as it sounds.

In a world where people are selling cupcakes on Instagram and earning in six figures, we can't keep preparing students to just fill answer sheets. If we want to build commerce graduates who don't get nervous when they see numbers, and who don't scroll through life without knowing how the internet actually works, then yes—Digital Marketing and Business Finance are not electives. They are essentials. Because in the modern business jungle, clicks and cash decide your survival.

In one line—what is your advice to commerce students who want to become entrepreneurs?

The result? A glorious mix of inspiration, sarcasm, and reality-checks—the kind only seasoned professors can deliver. One Sir said, *"Go to the field, experience market trends, and think uniquely."* In other words, stop Googling *"Top 5 start-up ideas in 2025"* and start walking around your own local market. Want to open a delivery business? Try delivering tiffins for a week first—not for Instagram, but for insight.

Another gem: *"Solve a societal problem, and your business will solve itself."* Too deep? Let's simplify. If your entire building is complaining about bad Wi-Fi, and you still start a candle-making business, maybe entrepreneurship isn't your calling yet. Look around. The next big idea might be sitting right under your neighbor's bad signal. Then came the classic old-school advice: *"Dedication, discipline, and hard work can make anything possible."* Yes, even if your only discipline right now is binge-watching motivational reels at 2 AM. Because let's face it—no entrepreneur succeeded by forwarding 'Good Morning' messages. They showed up, failed, fixed, and figured it out.

One teacher dropped a line that deserves a mic drop:

"With your commerce foundation, become the CEO of your own success." **Nice. But remember—you can't become a CEO if your only leadership experience is in deciding the chai tapri during break. Some teachers got real:** ***"Internships and on-ground experience are a must."*** **Why? Because sitting in a seminar and clapping for a guest**

speaker isn't "PRACTICAL LEARNING." Try standing behind a real counter for 3 days—you'll learn inventory, negotiation, and how customers can ask for change for ₹2000 even after buying something worth ₹15.

Another sir said, ***"Students think finance is important only when you're rich. But finance is what helps you get there."*** Truth bomb! Your passion won't survive three bad cash flow months. Learn how to budget. Or you'll be that guy who started a café and ended up drinking all the inventory himself.

One teacher added, ***"Take private skill courses. Degrees alone don't build empires."***

No one's going to invest in your start-up because you wrote 100 pages on Henry Fayol's principles. But if you know how to design a brochure, run an ad, and speak confidently that's gold. Let's not forget the boldest advice of them all.

"Don't be afraid to dream. And don't be afraid to take risks."

But please… calculated risks. Not the kind where you take ₹50,000 from your uncle and spend it all on a logo. And finally, the most teacher-ish (but honest) of all *"Commerce is the lifeline of the economy; entrepreneurial qualities must be nurtured seriously."*

In short, treat commerce like oxygen, not an optional subject. Because if you get it right, you won't just earn money — you'll create jobs, solve problems, and maybe even inspire the next chapter of someone else's story. So, dear student, stop asking *"Sir, is this answer enough for 5 marks?"* and start asking *"Sir, will this idea survive in the real market?"*

Start small. Fail fast. Learn quickly. Intern. Observe. Listen more than you speak. Because one day, your customer won't care about your grades, but they will care about your guts, your grit, and your guarantee.

So pick your dream.

Put on your shoes.

And let the real syllabus begin.

So yes, after all the chalk dust settled and all the attendance sheets were signed, our teachers gave us something far more valuable than notes—they gave us honesty. Their answers weren't dipped in sugar. They were dipped in sarcasm, wisdom, and the occasional frustration of checking 60 final-year projects titled "MY DREAM STARTUP"—none of which involved a real startup. They didn't ask for magic. They asked for logic. A little less "POWERPOINT" and a little more "POWER OF PRACTICE." A little less *"What is marketing?"* and a little more *"How do you sell a samosa during recess?"* One teacher even said, *"Give students ₹500 and let them feel what business is."* Another added, *"Our syllabus is still talking about fax machines… students are already on AI tools!"* The gap is not small—it's the size of a GST audit file. The funniest part? Everyone agrees students need more internships, real business practice, and exposure—but somehow, we still send them into the world with a file and a farewell. It's like teaching someone to ride a bike using only Google Slides—and then wondering why they fall at the first turn. And yet, there's hope. Real, strong hope. Because if teachers—who've been through it all—still believe that students can be turned into entrepreneurs with just a few real experiences, some creative space, and a change in attitude, then maybe, just maybe, we're not too late.

Because if there's one thing this chapter has made clear, it's this: Commerce education has the potential to change lives—but only when it stops acting like a textbook and starts behaving like a toolkit. Now that everyone's spoken—students, parents, society, and teachers—there's just one person left to speak. The one who's been writing all this, watching all this, and living all this for years.

The Voices Behind This Chapter:

The chapter *"Commerce Teachers Speak: Enough Theory, Let's Talk Reality"* has taken shape with the constant support, insights, and encouragement of several respected colleagues across institutions, and I wish to record my deepest gratitude to them. I am thankful to Shivam Tiwari of St. Joseph College of Arts and Commerce, Virar West, whose thoughtful inputs added clarity, and to Maqsood Hanif Memon of Sonopant Dandekar Arts, V.S. Apte Commerce and M.H. Mehta Science College, Palghar, whose academic guidance was invaluable. My sincere appreciation goes to Alisha Tuscano of St. Joseph College of Arts and Commerce, Virar West, and Dr. Deepa Lopes of Dnyandeep Mandal's St. Joseph College of Arts and Commerce, Arnala, Virar, for their enriching support and motivation. I also remain grateful to Dr. Kavita Robert Almeida of St. Joseph College of Arts and Commerce, Satpala, Rajodi Road, Virar West, for her valuable encouragement, and to Sahira Shah of Shah K.M. College of Commerce, Vasai, whose generous concern inspired me further. My heartfelt thanks extend to Sebastian Rebello of St. Gonsalo Garcia College of Arts and Commerce, Vasai, and to Prof. Dr. Vincent Kaitan D'Mello of St. Joseph College of Arts and Commerce, Satpala, Rajodi Road, Virar West, for their inspiring guidance and vision. I am equally indebted to Himali Chetan Page of SKC Degree College, Gass, Vasai, and Saritha Kurien of St. Gonsalo Garcia College of Arts and Commerce, Vasai West, for their thoughtful cooperation and encouragement. I gratefully acknowledge Bharat Mehta of Shah K.M. College of Commerce, Vasai, and Shahid Karim Memon of Anjuman-I-Islam Institute of Management Studies, Mumbai, for their motivating guidance, alongside Raut Prajakta Sharad of Abhinav College of Arts, Commerce and Science, Goddeo, Bhayander (E), Vasai, and Dr. Sanchita Datta of Royal College of Arts, Science and Commerce, Mumbai, for their meaningful contributions. I also extend warm appreciation to Lakshmi Muthukumar of SIES College, Sion West, Dr. Archana Devendra Joshi of Bhavan's College, Andheri West, Mumbai, and Sanjay Jagannath Bahare of Shri P. L. Shroff College of Arts and Commerce, Chinchani, Tal. Dahanu, for their unwavering support and scholarly guidance. Each of these distinguished individuals has, in their own way, helped shape this chapter into a more authentic, honest, and impactful dialogue, and I remain deeply grateful for their concern, cooperation, and belief in this work.

Turn the page, because in the next chapter, I speak.

And this time, I'm not holding back.

CHAPTER 10

THE FINAL BELL - VOICES THAT MATTER

From Reflection to Reform

In the last chapters, we heard voices—not just mine, but those of students, teachers, parents, and colleagues. Their questions, their confusion, and their honesty reminded us that commerce education isn't broken—it's simply lost direction. We've explored every classroom corner—students unsure why they even chose commerce, teachers stuck between passion and pressure, parents confusing safety with success, and policymakers who mean well but often miss the reality on the ground. Now, as I prepare to close this book, I feel a strong responsibility—not just to narrate what's wrong, but to suggest what could be right. This is not a conclusion.

This is a conversation starter.

So let me begin, as a teacher who's lived this system—with the most basic, yet most ignored issue in college life today: attendance.

Attendance: A Big Question for the Entire System.

Let's admit it—attendance today is more about adjustments than actual presence. I've seen classrooms where the teacher begins by calling roll numbers, but ends up calling out, *"Whose friend is here today?"* It's a system where one student attends, and five benefit. I once asked a boy why he doesn't attend regularly. He laughed and said, *"Sir, I have two friends—one for odd days, one for even days. My attendance is handled better than my bank account."* And teachers? We spend half our teaching time managing registers, Excel sheets, and last-minute reconciliations before inspection. *"Sir, this student was absent the whole month. How is he showing 80% attendance?"* The real comedy? Everyone knows it's fake—but everyone still plays along.

So here's my honest, implementable, no-nonsense suggestion:

A Centralized Biometric Attendance System.

Yes, biometric. One fingerprint. One scan. One central server. Directly controlled by the university—no college interference, no manual entries, no "ADJUSTMENTS." And to make it effective, let the degree carry a simple attendance tag:

Regular – for students who consistently attended

Flexible – for those who came and went like part-time interns

Correspondence – for those who practically disappeared

Now imagine an employer picking up a degree:

"B.Com – First Class – Flexible Attendance." Trust me,, that gives the employer an impression.

"B.Com – First Class – Regular." That speaks louder than any reference letter.

This system will bring transparency, honesty, and accountability.

No more faking presence. No more last-minute drama. Just pure data. As a teacher, this will save time. As a university, this will ensure fairness. And as a student, this will bring value to showing up not just on paper, but in person. Because at the end of the day, education only works when students are present physically, mentally, and purposefully.

Now, of course, this is just my suggestion. I'm not claiming it's a perfect solution, or that it will work like magic from day one. But as someone who has taught thousands of students and seen the classroom reality year after year, I genuinely feel that something like this can bring seriousness back into student life. Maybe it won't solve everything overnight. Maybe students will find ways around it too. But at least, it sends a message: *"Your presence matters. Not just for exams. But for life."* This is not about control. It's about clarity. Not about punishment. But about purpose. And if even a small change like this can make a student say, *"Let me attend it reflects on my degree,"* then I think it's worth trying. After all, not every idea needs to be perfect. But every system needs to be honest.

So yes, in my little dream world, this biometric system won't just mark attendance; it will classify students like Netflix categories. Some will proudly be "REGULAR" (the ones who actually warmed the college benches), some will be "FLEXIBLE" (the ones who treated college like a weekend hobby), and some will be "CORRESPONDENCE" (who

~ Education's purpose is to replace an empty mind with an open one.~ - ***Malcolm Forbes***

we last saw in the admission line). And the best part? Even an "IRREGULAR" student will have a valid reason: maybe they were working, maybe they were running a business so their employer will see, *"Ah, you weren't just bunking, you were hustling!"* This way, the degree tells a story, not just a percentage. Now, is this the perfect idea? Probably not. Many will call it overkill, some will call it genius, and a few will just call it *"Salim ka new drama."* But hey, it's just an idea, a spark.

And here's the real link: once attendance is honest and transparent, we can clearly see who actually belonged in the classroom and who didn't. This brings me to my next point: maybe it's time to let commerce choose its people.

Let Commerce Choose Its People

Let me now step back to the earlier part of this book where we heard real student stories.

Some entered commerce because their parents said it's "SAFE."

Some came because science felt scary.

Some joined because all their friends were joining.

And a few, just a few, chose commerce because they actually loved it.

Now tell me honestly how can a stream grow when most of its students never wanted to be there? I strongly believe that many of the problems we see in colleges today like low attendance, poor performance, and lack of interest begin right at the entry gate. Students who don't connect with commerce mentally will never commit to it physically. And when there's no connection, attendance becomes a burden, lectures feel boring, and assignments become last-minute Google copy-paste jobs.

Let me be blunt:

We don't need students who "LAND" in commerce. We need students who "BELONG" in commerce. I'm not denying that the New Education Policy (NEP) is a well-meaning reform. It promotes flexibility, student choice, and multi-disciplinary combinations, and that's a great step forward. But allow me to express a concern, not as a critic, but as a classroom teacher. When a student chooses commerce as a major and adds random subjects from science or arts just because it's "ALLOWED," we must ask: Is this student exploring, or simply confused? Imagine buying a car and then trying to attach a bike handle to it. Yes, it's possible. But it won't give you clarity, control, or comfort.

Similarly, if a student is taking commerce with unrelated subjects, they may become more confused, and worse, the employer will struggle to understand their skills. I'm not saying the NEP will fail. In fact, it might just work brilliantly for students who know what they want. But for most college students who are already lost, this flexibility could turn into a freedom to float aimlessly.

So here's my point:

Let's build a culture where commerce is offered, not as a default option but as a deliberate choice. Let school counsellors, teachers, and even parents ask students:

"Do you know what commerce is about?"

"Can you imagine yourself building a business, handling accounts, understanding markets?"

"Are you ready for the journey, not just the degree?"

And if the answer is no, that's okay!

Let them choose something else where their heart belongs, because commerce doesn't need numbers. It needs commitment. Just like law needs lawyers, and medicine needs doctors.

COMMERCE NEEDS COMMERCIAL MINDS.

Education Is Not for Sale!

Have you ever walked into a college and felt like you accidentally entered a warehouse? No proper classrooms, broken chairs, a half-working fan in the staff room, and a girls' common room that looks more like a leftover storeroom. And yet this place has university permission to run a full-fledged degree program. Sounds like a joke, right? But trust me, it's happening, a lot more than we think.

Let me tell you a real story that shook me.

A close friend of mine works at a college. One day, the campus was visited by the Local Inspection Committee (LIC) — those officials responsible for checking whether the college meets the standards. Within minutes, red flags were everywhere:

"There's no proper library."

"The staff room is barely functional."

"The girls' common room is non-existent."

"Playground? Not even a patch of grass."

I immediately said to my friend, *"This is serious. The college might get shut down."* But he just smiled calmly. And then he said something unforgettable: *"If all this is missing now, don't you think it was also missing when the college first got its permission? These buildings didn't fall apart overnight. They never existed in the first place."* That hit me hard. He was right. If the infrastructure was always this poor, then the real question is: Who gave the permission? And on what basis? What was the university or authority checking: actual facilities or just application files? Now here comes the next twist. In the same city, under the same university, I've seen some colleges with outstanding infrastructure—clean classrooms, full libraries, computer labs, auditoriums, and proper faculty cabins. And then just a few kilometers away, you find a college where even the water cooler is missing. How is that even possible? If all colleges are operating under one university, shouldn't there be uniform standards? Some kind of minimum benchmark? How can the same university allow one college to run with world-class facilities and another to barely function with broken benches and part-time staff? This isn't just inequality. This is negligence. Setting up a college should not be like opening a grocery store. But sadly, in many parts of India, it has become that easy.

All you need is:

A rented building,

A few second-hand chairs,

Some teachers on borrowed paperwork,

And a free lunch for the inspection team.

Suddenly, you're the "FOUNDER" of an educational institute.

Here's something even more shocking:

There are colleges that rent projectors, computers, and even library books just for the day of inspection. The next day, everything disappears along with the standards. According to UGC reports, over 20 fake universities were caught issuing degrees without approval, and that's just what we officially know. There could be hundreds more quietly operating behind glowing signboards and glossy brochures.

It's Clear:

A degree without delivery is not education. It's deception. We are producing graduates who don't know what they're supposed to know. Not because they're not smart, but because the system never gave them a real chance. Their college didn't teach — it just passed time. Their lectures didn't educate — they just filled hours. Their exams weren't about learning — they were about finishing.

This has to stop.

Universities must tighten inspections and standardize requirements. There should be minimum infrastructure norms across all affiliated colleges — non-negotiable, uncompromising. No library? No approval. No proper classrooms? No affiliation. No trained teachers? No business calling yourself a college. Because when the foundation of a college is weak, the future of its students will collapse. And when thousands of such students enter the market with half-baked knowledge and zero skills, it's not just their careers that suffer — it's the nation's growth that slows down.

Education is not a business plan.

It is a public responsibility.

It's time we treated it that way.

Let's stop giving licenses to buildings without soul,

and start empowering institutions with vision, ethics, and real infrastructure.

Because when we compromise on quality, we gamble with futures.

And in the name of education, that's the worst crime we can commit.

Teaching is Not Just a Job. It's a Nation-Building Mission.

Teaching is no longer just a profession; it is an ever-evolving, full-time responsibility. If anyone still believes that standing in class for four hours and going home is what teaching is about, they are seriously underestimating the system and insulting the soul of the profession. Today's teacher is not just a lecturer. They are a motivator, a counselor, a guide, a mentor, a tech user, a WhatsApp helpline, and sometimes, even a stand-in therapist during exam season. Getting to college on time? That's the easiest part of our day. The real journey begins after that: solving student doubts, attending meetings, creating question papers, setting answer keys, checking bundles of papers that all look like they were written by the same confused student using the same wrong formula in five different ways. And yet, we do it. Because we chose this life. Or maybe, this life chose us. We stand proudly under the sun on 15th August and 26th January while other professionals enjoy their public holiday in pajamas. Why? Because we don't celebrate the nation; we help build it. We accept that our profession will not always give us the highest salary, but it gives us the highest respect, provided we live up to it. Still, the reality is this: Teaching is no longer about chalk and duster. It's about change and direction. It requires constant innovation, relentless upgrading, and a mindset that embraces every new tool, from Google Meet to ChatGPT, not as threats, but as opportunities. And here comes the honest part: if you're uncomfortable with this change, if you think the old ways are good enough, then you may not belong in the new system. With folded hands and full respect to every teacher, I say this with love:

If you're here just because nothing else worked out, if teaching is your backup plan, or worse — a way to make quick money through side businesses and shortcuts — then please exit gracefully. Don't disrespect this sacred field by treating it like a pastime or a temporary hustle. Because this profession is not for survival. This is a profession that builds the survival skills of a whole generation.

A teacher doesn't just run a house.

A teacher runs a nation.

This is not a job you do from 10 to 4. This is a fire you carry every hour, every day, and every year. And now, allow me to close this chapter with one dream and one vision I carry deep in my heart: My dream teacher is not someone who just completes the syllabus on time. My dream teacher is someone who becomes such an inspiring figure that his own students feel proud to become a teacher. Because the day a student says, [sentence incomplete, missing quotation or conclusion]

"I want to become like my teacher,"

That day, education wins.

That day, the country wins.

And that, dear reader, is the teacher our system desperately needs.

If Education Were Like T20 Cricket…

Imagine asking today's 17-year-old to commit to six long years of education with a promise that *"something good will happen in the end."* That's like offering someone a boring documentary with the hope that the last five minutes might be fun. Sorry, sir, this is the T20 era. No one has that kind of patience. From fast food to fast apps to fast degrees (hello, online certificates!), everything today screams quick, effective, and exciting. And yet, our education system moves like it's in a slow-motion scene from a 90s family drama. Once upon a time, people watched five-day test matches with full devotion. Then came one-day cricket. Now it's T20: 3 hours, non-stop action, and thrilling results. Sadly, education is still stuck in the five-day match format. Students today are ready for T20-level learning. But what are we offering? Endless lectures, repeated notes, and exams that test memory instead of mindset. Now let's talk about the real problem: this six-year-long safari from SSC to graduation. It begins at age 15 or 16 and ends somewhere around 21. That's longer than most Netflix relationships. And in those six years, the mind doesn't just grow; it completely rewires itself. You ask a 16-year-old what they want to do, and they'll say, *"I want to be a graphic designer!"* Fast forward six years, and the same person is working in an insurance company, resizing passport photos in MS Paint. This isn't fiction, it's fact. I know a boy who said, *"Sir, I want to become a sports physiotherapist!"* He loved cricket, had studied human anatomy on YouTube, and even followed international trainers on Instagram. I met him five years later. Guess what he was doing? Auditing grocery bills in a CA firm. His passion didn't die. It just got bored waiting. Another student had dreams of opening a café. He was obsessed with latte art and banana-walnut muffins. Today, he sells financial products in a call center. Ask him about his dream, and he'll say, *"Sir, butter-paper pe likha tha… uda gaya."* This is what happens when education stretches for too long without direction. Dreams don't always die from rejection; they fade due to delay. The longer we make students wait, the more they begin to adjust, compromise, and finally forget.

So here's my proposal: Let's compress commerce education into a power-packed 2 or 3 years but with full-day engagement. Not 2 hours of boring lectures followed by 5 hours of chai and mobile scrolling. I'm talking about real engagement: half the day in classrooms, half the day in fieldwork, business projects, internships, and entrepreneurial labs. Give them a focused journey, not a long picnic with textbooks. You'll ask,

"But what about those who can't afford even this?" I'll ask you what they are doing now? Hanging around part-time jobs, wasting time, or stuck in family confusion. Let's offer scholarships. Let's build donation-based education clusters. Let's treat this as an investment in future taxpayers, not just temporary students.

We've already seen what six years of scattered learning produces confused graduates with a resume in one hand and a *"God knows what I'm doing"* look on their face. Instead, let's give them three years of purposeful preparation. Think about it. A student who enters commerce after SSC should be out of the system by age 19 or 20, ready for the industry or their own business. Whether their passion is sports, fashion, finance, or food, they should be allowed to pursue it with full force during those 2–3 years. Not as a "SIDE HUSTLE," but as a mainstream option. And here's the funniest part: Many students today learn more from Instagram reels than from their syllabus. A 60-second reel teaches them AI tools, editing apps, money-saving hacks, and branding tips. Meanwhile, their college lecture is stuck on *"What is barter system?"* Boss, we are trading time, not ideas.

Let me leave you with this thought. What if commerce education worked like a startup accelerator program? You enter with basic interest. You spend three years building projects, experimenting, failing, trying again. By the end, you come out either ready to join a company or start your own. No *"bonus semester."* No *"ATKT heartbreak."* Just practical, powerful, passion-filled learning. My idea may sound impractical to some. But so did the idea of remote jobs once.

So did the idea of learning coding on your phone. So did the idea of earning money through YouTube. And now, they're everyday realities.

So yes, this vision may feel ambitious. But if even 20% of this becomes reality, we won't just produce commerce graduates. We'll produce creators, thinkers, leaders, and doers all by the age of 20. And that, my friend, is a better ROI than any MBA can offer.

The NEP and Commerce Education: Between Dreams and Reality

"When one teaches, two learn." **– Robert Heinlein**

When we talk about the New Education Policy (NEP) today, it really does sound like a dream come true—practical projects, field assignments, and extra courses that prepare students for real-world skills. But recently, I heard some researchers ask a very practical question: *"How will all this actually work?"*

For example, there's a 30-hour skill course, and colleges get extra points for completing it. But the real question is: Do students really complete the full 30 hours? Or do they do just 15 hours and call it 30? I don't want to say every institution cheats, but unfortunately, many do things only for formality's sake. And if education becomes a formality, it's like bringing a spoon to a soup fight—not very useful! The NEP has introduced many exciting things—languages, sports, cultural activities, and lots of innovation. But here's the million-dollar question: Will the people who have to implement it actually do so properly? Implementation is the real challenge. Think about it like this: rules exist, but they often get broken—just like a driver without a license driving on the road. The NEP has created so many procedures that shortcuts almost seem inevitable in some colleges. Again, I am not saying every college cheats. But very often, the system and the people running it don't keep up.

The Key to Implementation

Imagine this: we gave a manual car driver a shiny new automatic car (that's the NEP), but we forgot to teach the driver how to use it properly. Teachers need to update their skills first. There have been countless seminars and meetings, but how many principals or teachers have really taken them seriously? If the implementers don't believe in the change, the system remains the same—just with smarter-looking PowerPoint slides. And here comes the funny (and sad) part: teachers. We expect them to give amazing results, but do we pay them well? Often not. In many colleges, if a qualified commerce teacher isn't available, anyone who is free becomes the "COMMERCE TEACHER." It's like hiring a chef to fix a car—technically possible but not a great idea!

Maharashtra-Specific Commerce Examples

In Mumbai, commerce students now have to complete a mandatory 120-hour internship in banks, financial firms, or startups—a big step toward real-world learning. One student (name withheld) landed an internship in an insurance firm and later got a trainee manager job, all thanks to this hands-on experience. But not all internship slots are of high quality. Some students joke that they got more credit for attendance than actual learning. Teachers in Maharashtra are also attending special NEP training sessions, sometimes even during exams, just to keep up. It's like telling students to study during holidays—challenging everywhere! Still, it shows effort is being made to bring NEP to life. Digital learning tools like DIKSHA and Maha-Swayam are also catching on. But in some colleges, teachers still use their own mobile data for online teaching. And Marathi-medium schools are adjusting to Hindi as a compulsory third language, preparing students for all-India business communication and laws. So yes, the NEP has big dreams and great plans. But whether those dreams come true depends on how seriously teachers, principals, and students take them. Otherwise, it's like buying a treadmill and using it as a clothes hanger!

Changing Student Attitudes

The NEP entered with great promise, like a beautifully planned wedding with colorful decorations, inspiring speeches, and the hope of a lifelong commitment. It spoke of transformation, flexibility, skill development, and student freedom. But if we peel back the glitter, the reality in many colleges is disappointing. As someone who teaches commerce at the university level, I've noticed a sharp shift—not in education delivery, but in student mentality. Admissions happen, yes. But students stop showing up after the first few days. It's as if college has become a place to register, not to learn. Attendance is low, classroom energy is missing, and the concept of regular lectures feels like a forgotten tradition. Ask students why they don't attend, and you'll hear: *"The lectures are boring,"* or *"We already know this,"* or worse, *"What's the point?"*

For many, college now feels like just a checkbox before moving on to "PRACTICAL" options: private diplomas, foreign universities, or online certifications. Some openly say they're only in college because their parents insisted. Even parents, sadly, no longer see value in lectures, events, or campus life. They're just waiting for that degree to arrive, preferably without much effort. Colleges, on the other hand, are trying to survive this decline like businesses in crisis. Some have turned into full-time marketing machines, advertising faculties, placements, and air-conditioned classrooms like they're selling a holiday package. It's become more about attracting students than educating them. It feels like institutions are hosting a grand party, but the guests aren't interested in dancing. Here's a fitting analogy: it feels like a wedding where everything is perfect: the flowers, the food, the outfits, but the bride and groom barely talk to each other. The marriage exists on paper, but there's no real connection. That's what's happening with NEP too. The policy looks great in documents, but the real relationship between education and students is fading.

Moving Forward with Hope

"Vision without action is merely a dream. Action without vision just passes the time. But vision with action can change the world." – Joel A. Barker

So, dear NEP authorities, your policy is strong, thoughtful, and much needed. Credit must be given where it's due. At least the conversation about reform has begun.

But we also need monitoring and accountability. Without it, this will become another case of *"policy in mind, but not in motion."* Many private institutes are already ignoring quality, opening shop, collecting fees, handing out degrees, with no one holding them accountable. If this continues, even a brilliant policy could silently fail.

Here are a few suggestions, straight from the classroom:

Use **centralized biometric attendance** so students can't fake their presence.

Classify degrees based on attendance and participation, so active learners earn more credible qualifications.

Regularly **inspect and audit** colleges, especially new ones.

Make sure college life isn't just about a degree, but about **building skills, confidence, and curiosity.**

Let's not allow another generation of students to walk out with a degree in hand but no vision in mind. Let's not treat college as a waiting room for adulthood. Education should be a launchpad, not a formality. Just like a meaningful marriage brings joy, growth, and lifelong learning, the journey of a commerce graduate should be full of discovery, excitement, and purpose. In the end, the NEP promises a new path for commerce students, mixing theory, skills, internships, and continuous assessments. The journey has bumps, yes, but also many success stories. As one student joked, *"In commerce, we're not just counting money; now, we're counting hours, credits, and sometimes even patience!"*

If students, teachers, and institutions embrace the spirit of NEP, not just its paperwork, then education in Maharashtra and India can truly transform. Because education, like a good Bollywood movie, deserves not only drama and suspense, but also a happy ending.

But before I end, let me share something very personal — an experience that changed me as a student and later guided me as a teacher. Reforms, policies, and systems are important, yes. But sometimes, it is a simple activity, a camp, or a teacher's vision that changes a student's entire outlook. And I know this because it happened to me.

The Camp That Changed My Fear into Confidence

Before I close this book, let me take you back to my own college days — because reforms, policies, and systems matter, yes, but sometimes it is a single experience that changes a student's life forever. For me, that moment came in my very first year of B.Com at St. Gonsalo Garcia College, Vasai. Like every other commerce student, I thought college meant lectures, boring notes, and occasional picnics. Then one day came an announcement:

"All students must attend a three-day Personality Development Camp."

I rolled my eyes. *"What new torture is this? Can personality really be taught in three days?"* I muttered to my friend. To me, camps meant watery tea and endless queues, not life lessons. But since it was compulsory, I had no choice. Half interested, half irritated, I packed my bag and went.

What happened next was nothing less than magic.

A Camp That Opened My Eyes

The camp was led by Father Patrick, a visionary teacher who always said:

"Books give you knowledge, but activities give you courage."

The very first session felt strange. Students were asked to sit together and share the pain hidden in their hearts. Some cried while speaking about failures or family struggles. Some sang songs to express their emotions. At first, I thought, *"Is this college or a therapy center?"* But as I listened, I realized something powerful every student carries hidden fears, pressures, and dreams. Then came an activity called *"One-to-One Correspondence."* A boy and a girl, complete strangers, had to sit far apart and talk for thirty minutes. Imagine me, a shy FY B.Com student, suddenly asked to speak to a girl I had never seen before! My heart raced faster than an LIC premium reminder. But when I finally spoke, something broke inside me my fear. Later, we had to share our experiences on stage, holding the mic. For the first time in my life, I spoke in front of everyone. My legs shook like a student whose accounting balance didn't tally, but my voice came out strong. When the audience clapped, I felt something priceless confidence.

Out of Comfort Zone, Into Real Growth

Over the next two days, we had role-plays, songs, dances, and comedy acts. Boys who were silent in class became stage stars. Girls who always hid in the back came forward with powerful speeches. And I? I discovered a side of myself I never knew existed. That camp didn't just give us fun. It gave us freedom. It showed us that personality is not taught in textbooks it is built through experiences. If college had not forced me into that camp, maybe I would still be the boy afraid to talk to strangers, afraid to take the mic. But because of those three days, I discovered my voice.

Why Every College Needs a Father Patrick

Looking back, I feel every student deserves a Father Patrick a teacher who goes beyond lectures, who believes that education is not just about clearing exams but about shaping lives.

Because the truth is this: commerce education gives you time, but it doesn't tell you how to use it. Camps like these fill that gap. They make you face your fears, polish your confidence, and reveal your hidden talents. I tell my students even today, *"If such activities happen in your college, never bunk them. These are the real classes where you discover yourself."* And if your college doesn't offer them? Then chase teachers who think differently. Join activities. Create your own stage. Because one day, when life puts the mic in your hand, you should not stand silently.

A Promise for the New Vision of Education

That camp taught me a lesson that has stayed forever. Education without personality development is like a pizza without toppings, flat and forgettable. We need camps, workshops, and creative activities in the new vision of education, because marks may give you a degree, but personality gives you respect, opportunities, and the courage to face life. So yes, my degree gave me knowledge. But those three camp days gave me courage, friends, and a voice that I still carry with me. And that, I believe, is what the future of education must ensure for every child.

~Education's purpose is to replace an empty mind with an open one.~ - ***Malcolm Forbes***

Exams may test your memory, but activities test your courage.

And courage, not marks, is what truly shapes your future.

Final Note from the Author

Now that the book is coming to an end, I feel like a teacher at the end of the academic year — relieved, emotional, and hoping the message has reached the backbenchers too! Let me start with what inspired this book. In the earlier chapters, I shared real-life stories of students who struggled, of teachers who tried, and of a system that kept running even when the wheels were broken. These stories were not fictional or borrowed from some news article. They were personal. I have lived them. Observed them. Taught through them. The purpose was never to blame anyone. It was to reflect the true mindset of our students, teachers, and policymakers. The noble profession of education, which was once seen as a service to society, has sadly been treated as a business model by many. Those who are smart and capable have started making money out of it, while those with real passion are left buried under low pay, outdated systems, and back-to-back Diwali, Christmas, and summer vacations. Honestly, in some places, the only consistent thing in education is the number of holidays. Commerce, as a stream, has great potential. But somewhere along the way, it got reduced to a backup option — a plan B for those who didn't get into engineering or medicine. Despite its huge success in producing professionals, it's not giving the output we expected. Why? Because the system is being run like a movie where 5–6 great directors are involved, each trying to pull the story in a different direction, but no one is able to bring it to a good climax.

This book is not written by a revolutionary or a bestselling author. It's written by a simple commerce teacher — someone who has spent more time in classrooms than on vacation. Someone who has seen talented students give up, good teachers get ignored, and policies made without asking the people on the ground. It's written out of pure passion… and maybe a bit of helplessness. I remember being invited to multiple university meetings to discuss syllabus changes. Everyone was allowed to speak, but the final syllabus was always decided by the front row — the policymakers while the rest of us clapped politely. Once, we were asked for our opinion on changing the textbook. I gave 10 solid points. Later, I found the new textbook had only one change: the price. The business of selling books and online courses in the name of "SYLLABUS REFORM" has become unstoppable. Education has now become a market. Some colleges run it nationally. Some have expanded internationally. But somewhere, the aim has been lost. NEP can bring direction, yes, but implementation still lies in the hands of the same old story makers — our parents, students, and policymakers.

And so, before I end, I want to leave this book with 4 small but strong requests:

To Teachers : **If you are passionate, become a teacher — not for holidays or backup** income. Teach because you care.

To Students : If you truly love commerce, then pursue it. Not because it's easy or convenient, but because it's powerful.

To Policy Makers : Please don't treat education like a business pitch. Reform is not a brochure **It's a responsibility.**

To Parents : **Don't treat your children as an investment. They're not stocks to give returns.** returns. They're stories waiting to be written.

To My Readers : This is my first book. It may not be perfect, but it is honest. It carries my real experiences, my classroom stories, and those sleepless nights when I kept asking myself, *"Will things ever change?"* If these pages can bring even a small shift, if one student dares to ask "Why," if one parent pauses before pushing a child, or if one policymaker thinks twice before signing a syllabus, then I feel my role as a teacher is fulfilled, because in the end, education is not only about giving a degree — it is about giving a vision.

Let's build a world where students don't just get a DEGREE, but they get a VISION TOO.

Thank you for reading.

– Dr. Salim Karim Memon

GRATITUDE FOR CONTRIBUTION

Every dream needs people who believe in it — who question, inspire, and shape it with their own light. "DEGREE IN HAND, VISION ON HOLD: REDEFINING COMMERCE EDUCATION" is not just my book; it's a journey that carries the thoughts, energy, and spirit of many incredible individuals who stood beside me.

I am deeply thankful to Prof. Dr. Vincent Kaitan D'Mello, Dr. Deepa Lopes, Dr. Kavita Robert Almeida, Dr. Sanchita Datta, Dr. Archana Devendra Joshi, Dr. Subhash Dsouza, and Dr. Dinesh Sanadhi — your academic wisdom and constant motivation kept the vision of this book focused and strong.

To my friends and well-wishers — Javed Karim Memon, Wajid Ismail Memon, Shafique Memon, Shivam Tiwari, Maqsood Hanif Memon, Alisha Tuscano, Sahira Shah, Sebastian Rebello, Himali Chetan Page, Saritha Kurien, Bharat Mehta, Shahid Karim Memon, Raut Prajakta Sharad, Lakshmi

Muthukumar, Sanjay Jagannath Bahare, Saeed Patel, Nikita Prabhu, Priya Telkar, Jaspreet Kaur, Sneha Gupta, Amrita Tiwari, Kanishka Tiwari, Kritika Chaurasiya, Parveen Beg, Alpana Mahale, Danish Khan, Sandeep Gonsalves, Shalini Dube, Jane Rodrigues, Noel Sir, Mr. Riaz Mulla, Abdul Shaikh, Fatima Shaikh, Sandesh Shetty, Dhaval Rathod, Raj Shah, Dhaval Shah, Sanjay Gupta, Divyank Chauhan, Abhishek Sharma, Jeenal Gandhi and Gabriel N. Jhon — each of you has touched this book in your own special way.

Whether through a discussion that sparked a new thought, a story that added emotion, or simply a word of encouragement when it was needed most — your contribution has made this book come alive. You have given not just your time, but your heart.

This acknowledgment is more than a thank you — it is a celebration of your presence in this mission to rethink commerce education. Together, we've proved that when minds unite for a purpose, ideas become movements.

With genuine happiness and deep gratitude,

Dr. Salim Karim Memon

WITH HEARTFELT GRATITUDE TO OUR SUPPORTERS